LIZARD CARE
FROM A TO Z

Second Edition

R. D. Bartlett & Patricia Bartlett

BARRON'S

About the Authors

R. D. Bartlett is a herpetologist who has authored hundreds of articles and numerous books, as well as co-authored many other books. He lectures extensively and has participated in field studies across North and South America. Patricia Bartlett is a biologist and historian who has also authored and co-authored numerous books. In 1970 the Bartletts began the Reptilian Breeding and Research Institute, a private facility. Since its inception, hundreds of reptilian and amphibian species have been bred at the facility, some for the first time in the United States under captive conditions.

All inquiries should be addressed to:
Barron's Educational Series, Inc.
250 Wireless Boulevard
Hauppauge, New York 11788
www.barronseduc.com

Library of Congress Catalog Card No. 2008008533

ISBN-13: 978-0-7641-3890-4
ISBN-10: 0-7641-3890-1

Library of Congress Cataloging-in-Publication Data
Bartlett, Richard D., 1938–
   Lizard care from A to Z / R. D. Bartlett and Patricia Bartlett. — 2nd ed.
      p.   cm.
   Includes bibliographical references and index.
   ISBN-13: 978-0-7641-3890-4
   ISBN-10: 0-7641-3890-1
   1. Lizards as pets. I. Bartlett, Patricia Pope, 1949–
II. Title.

   S459.L5B37   2008
   639.3′95—dc22   2008008533

Printed in China
9 8 7 6 5 4 3 2 1

Photo Credits

All photos by R. D. and Patricia Bartlett.

Cover Photos

All photos by R. D. and Patricia Bartlett.

Acknowledgments

Over the years, we've talked with and listened to many herpetologists. Their knowledge has been incorporated into this book of lizard husbandry. To all, we owe a debt of gratitude.

Bill Love and Rob MacInnes have provided us with quantities of information as well as unparalleled photographic opportunities. Chris McQuade has indulged our photographic whims. Jim Harding, Regis Opferman, Mike Souza, Tom Tyning, Ernie Wagner, and Kenny Wray have offered comments for this project as well as companionship in the field. Randy Gray and Matthew Moyle have provided expertise on the spiny-tailed agamids. Bert and Hester Langerwerf have shared many of their techniques on lizard husbandry. Yvette Frey has offered her thoughts on iguana care. Billy Griswold and Karin Burns have provided thoughts on bearded dragon husbandry, lizards with which they have been particularly successful. Although our chart on medicine was provided by Richard Funk, D.V.M., we also owe our sincerest thanks to Frederic Frye, D.V.M., for his comments.

Important Note
This book tells the reader how to care for lizards. The author and publisher consider it important to point out that the advice given in this book is meant primarily for normally developed lizards of excellent physical health.

If you are scratched or bitten by a lizard, you should consult a physician. Caution is advised in the association of children or pets with lizards.

Lizards may do damage to someone else's property or cause accidents. It is therefore in the owner's interest to be adequately insured against such eventualities, and we strongly urge all lizard owners to purchase a liability policy that covers their pets.

Contents

Preface

This book is designed to help you with the care of all lizards commonly seen today in America's pet marketplace. It includes husbandry and dietary information for green iguanas and other herbivores; blue-tongued skinks and other omnivores; monitors, tegus, and other carnivores; geckos and other insectivores. Our problem is not whether we can fill these pages but, rather, what we can leave out and still provide you with somewhat more than the basics.

Sadly, the husbandry of lizards remains fraught with misconceptions—erroneous suppositions—and actual misinformation is passed on by well-meaning persons who are relying on outdated conventional wisdom.

One particular example that we hope you will notice is the dietary necessities of the immensely popular green iguanas. While the answers to certain questions remain unknown, we *do* know that iguanas held in captivity respond differently to certain dietary items than wild examples do. Animal protein such as monkey chow, insects, and mice is usually harmful to these "reptilian cows." Daily feedings of a combination of fresh veggies (no spinach, please), some blossoms, and a few pieces of ripe fruit (to which is added some vitamin D_3 and calcium) creates a healthy diet that will allow your pet the chance to live out its normal lifespan of 10 to 20 years!

We have long known that lizards are ectotherms (cold-blooded) but we now know that rather than leading lackadaisical, humdrum lives, lizards are alert, active, and continually interacting with others of their own kind. The range of a few lizard species enters the Arctic Circle in the north and Tierra del Fuego in the south, but most are of tropical distribution. Even some of those tropical forms dwell in the comparative coolness of montane habitats, and warm themselves by basking. Others that dwell in the heat of the desert must strive to remain cool, lest they die.

Many lizards are available to hobbyists. To those we choose to keep, we owe the debt of knowledge of their needs. To those that are so difficult that they can't be readily kept, we owe the debt of continued freedom.

Dick and Patti Bartlett

Introduction

Although hobbyists have been maintaining lizards for years, these animals, as a group, remain more poorly understood than snakes. Snakes can be kept and will breed in relatively tiny, dimly lit containers, while lizards, for the most part, would quickly decline under that type of care. In captivity lizards require spacious quarters with bright, full-spectrum lighting and careful attention to a diet that includes a balanced blend of vitamin and mineral supplements. Almost equally great attention must be paid to the microhabitat (see page 10) in the caging. In short, most lizards are more difficult to keep than most snakes, and, despite the fact that hobbyists *have* been keeping lizards for years, we know much less about many of them (including some mainstays of the pet industry) than we do about snakes.

But we are learning. In the past few years veterinary knowledge of lizards and their health problems has increased exponentially. Veterinarians and herpetoculturists have become aware that diagnoses and treatment of reptile ailments may differ substantially from those of more traditional warm-blooded pets. Today, if the lizards of many species are in fair to good condition when we obtain them, we *can* keep them alive. If we get a pair, and provide caging conditions to their liking, we have at least a fair chance at captive reproduction.

Captive breeding of lizards will become more important with each passing year. Wild populations of many species are diminishing due to one or combined factors. Many countries are invoking strong conservation laws disallowing the collection and exportation of lizards for the pet trade. If, in the future, we hope to have access to species that we see today, we must learn to breed them.

We are succeeding with some: green iguanas are now being captive bred in ever increasing numbers. True chameleons, all species of which we have long considered problematic, are finally yielding their secrets to us. There are successful programs for day geckos and blue-tongued skinks, monitors and spiny-tailed agamids, and other species. Sadly, but not unexpectedly, we now know more about the needs of many rare and expensive species than about those of some common forms. This is a clear instance of "money talking." When

1

A male dwarf Jackson's chameleon, Chamaeleo jacksonii merumontanus, *descends a limb.*

financial returns are high, there is more incentive.

Most of us start out by acquiring an anole or fence lizard collected from our garden or purchased for a couple of dollars from a neighborhood pet store. If we (and the lizard) are lucky, we'll have already learned about some of its needs by watching it in the wild, by reading about lizards, or by being given some minimal instructions on lizard care by shop personnel.

Ideally, the lizard will do well and live a normal lifespan, but this is often not the case. It is more likely that the lizard will *seem* to thrive, then begin an inexorable decline. The decline can result from the cumulative effects of incorrect lighting, suboptimal cage temperatures, vitamin-mineral imbalance, insufficient nourishment, incorrect watering techniques, or actual illness. Lizards are slow to show a decline in health. By the time poor health is advanced enough to have manifested itself externally, it may well be too late to save the creature.

Do remember that none of these creatures asked to be taken captive. It is our responsibility to provide all, whether a two-dollar five-lined skink or a $5,000 perentie monitor, with optimal care and to be ready to finance veterinary intervention if necessary.

It is our intent here to familiarize you with the regimen of necessary care—with methods that have worked for us—but to emphasize that these are examples only. These are *not* the *only* methods that will work. What seems ideal in one part of the country (or world) may not work as well in another. If you live in a humid area you may need to reduce the relative humidity in a cage. If you live in an arid area you may need to increase the cage humidity for certain species. If you live in the southern tier states you may need to cool your cages in summer; if you live in Alaska it may be necessary to heat your cages year round. We urge you to use our comments as guidelines and to develop the regimen necessary for success in your region.

Chapter One
Keeping Your Lizards

Hobby Versus Commercialism, Herpetology Versus Herpetoculture

Let's define our terms: What is herpetology and what is herpetoculture?

Herpetology is the study of reptiles and amphibians. The subjects involved include, but are not limited to, classification, natural history, anatomy, and behavior. The researchers are usually schooled in the science and are termed *herpetologists*.

Herpetoculture, on the other hand, is the hobby of keeping and breeding reptiles and amphibians. The individuals involved, whether professionals or nonprofessionals, are *herpetoculturists.*

And while we're at it, what does *herptile* mean? In his *Dictionary of Herpetology* (1964), James A. Peters gives a terse definition: "A completely illegitimate term that has been used recently in amateur literature as a short-hand reference to reptiles and amphibians. It is also occasionally used in professional literature by authors who apparently lack a classical background." Now, some 30-plus years later, the term is still used and it still identifies the user as a rank beginner. Even though more burdensome, it is better to say "reptiles and/or amphibians," or in a pinch, "herps."

Herpetoculture has progressed both in the collections of zoological gardens and in the private sector. In fact, the success of the private sector has, at times, seemed to surpass that of zoos.

Although it may seem a giant step to a newcomer to the hobby, the difference between herpetoculture as a hobby and herpetoculture as a business is not great. As a hobbyist gains more expertise, the natural progression is to first develop a breeding program, then to increase its scope. A program may include only one, or may include several species.

When they first begin breeding lizards on a small scale, hobbyists are often referred to as "backyard breeders." Because these small-scale breeders often sell the offspring they produce for far less than a commercial breeder, the term is not entirely complimentary.

Herpetoculture may work as a conservation tool, for when captive-bred specimens are available in suitable numbers, it is less necessary to collect wild specimens to supply a seemingly insatiable pet trade. In today's world of diminishing wild areas and reduced numbers of wildlife, this is an important consideration. However, a second conservation argument, that of re-releasing into the wild captive-born progeny to increase wild populations, is really not valid. Actually, it has been shown on numerous occasions that released long-term and captive-bred reptiles do not do well. In fact, while attempting to establish a territory, an introduced lizard may upset the natural equilibrium of an established population. Because of pathogens they harbor, released reptiles may actually have a significant negative impact on wild populations. Released reptiles may tax an already stressed ecosystem.

In other words, once captive, your lizards, and their progeny, should remain so.

The Name Game

At some time in your lizard-keeping career, you will probably visit a number of pet shops or look over the lists of mail order dealers. You will probably note that the same lizard may have different names in different shops or on the dealers' lists. We call this the name game and we find it as aggravating as you will. How can the names of the same lizards vary? And what do those other names—the hard-to-pronounce ones on the dealer's list—mean?

Let's take the last question first, for even though more unsettled now than ever before, those hard-to-pronounce names are the scientific names, and they should be the ones in which you are most interested.

Scientific names have resulted from man's need to categorize—to give order and a degree of unity to the plants and animals that surround us. This is the science of *taxonomy*.

The Linnaean System

Credit for our present system, the Linnaean system of binomial nomenclature, goes to the eighteenth-century Swedish botanist Carl (Carolus) Linnaeus (von Linne), a man not at all fond of herpetofauna. His first compilation of names appeared in 1735 in a publication entitled *Systema Naturae.*

Despised by some of his colleagues for its "artificiality," Linnaeus' system of binomial nomenclature based on appearance and characteristics nonetheless began an era of comparative nomenclatural stability. This system is often referred to by taxonomists as "traditional systematics." (A second method of classification—"cladistics"—is altering the method of classification within the system.) Today, we also recognize subspecies, necessitating *tri*nomial listings.

The Linnaean system of classification works very much as our own names do, but the names used are based on Greek or Latin origins. The scientific names are always differentiated from surrounding text by underscoring, italicizing, or, if used in an italicized text, by non-italicizing. The scientific names are always the same and are readily recognized by herpetologists and advanced herpetoculturists throughout the world.

Using the nominate (first described) subspecies of a North American chuckwalla, *Sauromalus obesus obesus,* as an example, we have the following:

Sauromalus (always capitalized and, if repeated, usually abbreviated to the first letter, still capitalized, followed by a period) is the genus name. This equates to your surname. A genus (plural, genera) is defined as "a group of species having similar structural characteristics."

The second word, *obesus,* designates the species. It is defined as "a group of similar organisms that are able to interbreed and produce viable offspring." The species name is not capitalized but, once written out, if followed by a subspecific name, it may be abbreviated to its first letter and a period, such as *o.*

If, across its range, a species is identical, the nomenclature stops right there, hence the name is a *binomial.* However, if the species differs geographically in pattern, coloration, scalation, etc., yet the ranges are or were contiguous and populational interbreeding remains possible, a subspecies, or race, may be designated. In these cases

Once a species with several subspecies, current taxonomic principals have consolidated the common chuckwalla into a single form, Sauromalus ater.

a subspecific name is given. This is the third word of the name that has then become a *trinomial.*

The third word in our example was *obesus.* Not only did the presence of that third word inform us that the chuckwalla has more than a single identifiable subspecies but, in its redundancy, the trinomial indicated that that form, commonly referred to as the western chuckwalla, was the first (the nominate type) to be described.

Common names are anything but standardized. For instance, one species of *Uromastyx* from the Middle East may be called a "dabb lizard," a uromastyx, a spiny-tailed agamid, or the diminutive of "uro." It may also be referred to as a desert spiny-tailed lizard, a Morocco spiny-tail, or a Saharan dabb lizard. Or it may be called by any combination of these names. It might be known by one common name in one pet store, and a very different common name

5

in another. And if the lizard doesn't sell well under one common name this week, a canny dealer just might change its name on next week's list! The bottom line is that scientific names are the more reliable.

Knowing the scientific name of the specimen you are hoping to buy becomes even more critical when you are ordering a rarity, sight unseen, by mail order.

Why would you do this? Read on.

Obtaining Your Lizards

Location Is Important

Although the hobby of keeping reptiles is, of course, not limited to any one section of the United States, Europe, or Asia, the commercial availability of reptiles is better in some regions of those countries than in others.

In the United States, the major reptile dealers are in California, Florida, and New York. From airports in the larger cities in these states, reptiles are air freighted to wholesalers who supply pet shops and, in some cases, herpetocultural breeders. There is usually some overlap among these businesses.

Pet shops may be able to provide information on the lizards they sell, but in most cases they rely on their wholesaler for information.

There are some things you cannot expect your local pet shop to know, such as the exact geographical origin of a given wild-collected specimen or the genetics of captive-bred specimens. Remember, your local pet shop is often two or even three or four times removed from the source of the specimen.

The growth in popularity of reptiles has created the specialty dealers. A specialty dealer concentrates on the sale of reptiles and often is better able to answer your questions. The imported lizards are usually acclimated, have been fed, and, often provided a veterinary checkup. It is from the specialty dealers that the greatest variety of lizards is usually available.

Breeders are one of the best sources of parasite-free, well-acclimated specimens, and accurate information. Most breeders keep records of genetics, lineage, fecundity, health, and the quirks of the lizards with which they work. Their records are invariably available to their customers.

Shipping

The lizard(s) you seek may be available only from a dealer or breeder at some distance from you. In this case, you'll need to drive to the dealer or breeder or have the lizards shipped to you by air. Your supplier will be familiar with shipping and will be only too happy to ship to you.

There are a few things you need to think about when air transportation is involved:

• You generally pay for the animal and the shipping charges in advance. Your shipper will need your credit card number and expiration date, a money order, or a cashier's check. Many shippers will accept personal checks but wait until the check clears the bank before shipping (usually within a week or so).

- Another payment method is COD; however, this can be expensive and inconvenient. Most dealers will hesitate to send a package COD; if you have the money, they reason, why can't you get a cashier's check? Airlines will accept cash only for the COD amount and there is a hefty collection ($15.00 or more) fee, in addition to all other charges.
- Give your supplier your full name, address, and current day *and* night telephone numbers where you can be reached.
- Inform your shipper of the airport you wish to use, or agree on a door-to-door delivery company. If your area is serviced by more than one airport (such as the Washington D.C. or San Francisco, California areas), be very specific about the airport.
- Agree on a shipping date and on that date call your supplier for the airbill number. Some shippers go to the airport on one or two specific days each week. Avoid weekend arrivals when the cargo offices at most small airports are closed.
- Allow enough time for your shipment to get to you before panicking. Most shipments take about 24 hours to get from the airport of origin to the airport of destination.

- Keep your shipment on the same airline whenever possible; with live animals you pay for each airline involved.
- Ship only during "good" weather. Your lizard may be delayed when the weather is very hot, very cold, or during the peak holiday travel/shipping/mailing times.
- Most airlines offer three choices: regular "space available" freight (this is the most frequently used and the suggested service level), air express (guaranteed flights), or small package (the fastest level of service). You will pay premium prices for either of the last two levels but they may be required by the airline if shipping conditions are adverse. Compare airlines. Some carriers charge a lot more than others for the same level of service.
- After a reasonable time, call the airline that your shipment is traveling on and ask them for the status of the shipment. The airline will need the airbill number to trace the shipment in its computer.

Lizards now available in the pet trade are imported from worldwide sources.

Open your shipment at the air cargo office to determine the condition of the lizards.

All of the above may seem complex, but using air freight is a very simple and comparatively fast way to ship lizards.

Collecting Them Yourself

Rather than purchasing our lizards, some of us prefer to collect them ourselves. Many states within the United States, and several European countries, have rather strict conservation policies that require specific permits for collecting or keeping native species. Other states may require that a fishing or hunting license be purchased prior to any collecting and they limit the number of any given species that can be collected or kept. Collecting regulations may be different for nonresidents of an area than for residents. Still other areas may have no regulations at all. Research all pertinent regulations carefully and abide by all equally carefully.

If those lizards in which you are interested are found near your home—and it is legal to collect them—it is usually an easy matter to do so. Find out about that lizard, the time of year that it is most active and easily observable, and if it changes habitats with the seasons. For example, knight and Jamaican giant anoles are canopy dwellers during the cooler months (where they are difficult to find and collect) but descend to the lower trunks when the weather warms. They are, of course, more easily found during the times they are closest to the ground.

- Pick your shipment up as quickly after its arrival as possible. This is especially important in bad weather. Learn the hours of your cargo office and whether the shipment can be picked up at the ticket counter if it arrives after the cargo office has closed.
- Once the airline has checked that your shipment has been paid for, you'll be able to inspect it. Open and inspect it before leaving the cargo facility. Unless otherwise specified, reliable shippers guarantee live delivery; however, if there is a problem, both the shipper and the airline(s), will require a "discrepancy" or "damage" report made out, signed, and dated by airline cargo personnel. In the very rare case when a problem occurs, insist on the filling and filing of a claim form right then and contact your shipper *immediately* for instructions.

If finding the lizards in which you are interested requires rolling logs or otherwise disturbing the environment, be sure to alter the area as little as possible. Replace all rocks, logs, fronds, or other cover after searching. Capture only the number of lizards with which you wish to work and do not alter the environment while you are afield.

Once collected, transport the lizard safely, protecting it from excesses of heat or cold. Small lizards can be transported in covered plastic deli cups. Larger specimens can be transported in tightly tied cloth bags.

If the specimens are humidity-loving anoles or broad-headed skinks, a *barely* dampened crumpled paper towel should be placed in the cup or bag with them. If they are desert dwellers, the paper towel should still be used, but it should be dry.

In all cases, get the lizards to their permanent cages as quickly as possible.

Know the Conservation Laws

Lizards, and all other reptiles and amphibians, are increasingly protected by conservation laws. The laws of each state may differ widely in content or application. Prior to collecting any lizards from the wild, ascertain that it is legal to do so. To do this we strongly recommend

When transporting lizards that require moisture, such as this Chinese glass lizard, Ophisaurus hartii, *add a crumpled, moistened paper towel before knotting the carrying bag.*

that you check the laws of the state game and fisheries commissions where you hope to collect your lizards. Also familiarize yourself with intermeshing federal laws by requesting information from the federal government's Department of the Interior. Penalties for breach of the laws (which can apply not only to collecting, but to transportation and sale/purchase of various species as well) can be severe. Know the laws and remember that laws change and it is your responsibility to remain current. Ignorance is not an excuse, nor would ignorance be a defense for a responsible hobbyist. (John Levell has recently written *A Field Guide to Reptiles and the Law,* a book that will help you remain abreast of applicable state and federal regulations.)

Chapter Two
Caging

The Importance of Knowing the Range

The range of a lizard—where it can be found in the world—will tell you what type of caging to provide. For instance, knowing that a lizard is indigenous to the western United States will save you from looking for information in an eastern field guide, just as knowing that a given species is found in England will start you toward a guide of Great Britain and Europe rather than one of Africa. Thus, the range of a species is important.

Latitudinal ranges: Knowing the latitudes within which a species occurs is also important. Generally, ambient cage temperatures will be different for lizards found at the latitude of Washington State and British Columbia than for those that range through southern Arizona and northern Mexico.

But there's another factor you need to consider:

Elevational ranges: Now that you have found the latitude at which the lizard you are researching occurs, try to determine its preferred elevational range. The ambient temperature that a lizard would have to contend with would be very different on the desert floor of Death Valley, California, 280 feet (85 m) below sea level, than it would on the wooded slopes of Sherman Peak, California, which rises some 9,900 feet (2,743 m) above sea level, yet both places are at the same latitude.

Habitats: Of course, habitats make a big difference! You sure wouldn't expect to find a montane (mountain dwelling) Mt. Kenya Jackson's chameleon, a species of cool, rainy, forested slopes, on the open treeless expanses of the Serengeti. Nor would you have success looking for a desert sand-dwelling fringe-toed lizard in areas of clinging clay substrate. Find out what the habitat is for your particular lizard.

Microhabitats: Microhabitat is a more specific habitat description. Does your desert-dwelling lizard prefer the open, hotter, drier stretches of desert like a desert iguana, or is it restricted to areas that retain at least a vestige of moisture—under rocks, in decomposing plant material, along river and stream edges—like many of the skinks? Defining these variables

The terrarium or cage must be designed to fit the needs of the lizards. Shield-tailed agamas, Xenagama taylori, *for example, require a rocky desert terrarium. When content, dominant male* X. taylori *develop an intense blue coloration on the snout, throat, and chest.*

will help you even more in providing the terrarium conditions most suitable for the long-term comfort of your lizard.

Design of the Terraria and Cages

Tailor the design of your terraria and cages to the needs of your lizards. Provide arboreal lizards with vertical cages and terrestrial species with terraria of horizontal design. Orientation is more important when cages are small than when they are large. Terraria may be adapted from readily available pet shop aquaria, made from glass, from wire, wood-framed, from sheet aluminum, or in any number of other ways. They may vary in cost from relatively inexpensive (small commercial aquaria for small

lizards) to quite extravagant in both design and cost. Expensive does not necessarily equate with better. It is how they are set up for the species they are to house that counts most.

Some lizards are far less agile than others. Terrestrial species such as blue-tongued skinks and sungazers neither jump nor climb well and are also comparatively slow. These may be kept in open-topped pens of only reasonable depth. Other lizards (iguanas, monitors) are fast and agile and can climb and jump. These require far more secure cages.

Because they are so readily available in the pet trade, the purchase of a green iguana, large monitor, tegu, or other large lizard species by a new hobbyist is all too often an impulse purchase. It is hard for even those of us who have seen and handled adult iguanas and monitors to

Where climatic conditions allow, large lizard cages can be built outdoors.

visualize the changes that occur with growth. Along with the increase in size is the fact that a lizard's disposition may change once it reaches sexual maturity. This is especially true of males.

Young male iguanas, monitors, and tegus can be housed communally, but adults cannot. Males stake out and defend their territories against other males of their species. Females are usually much less territorial; if adequate space is given, they can usually be housed communally, or with a single male, throughout their lives.

From space considerations alone, smaller lizard species are easier to house at all stages of their life than larger species. Equally easily understood is the fact that, if you

want to keep medium-to-large lizard species, aridland and savanna dwellers are more easily housed than persistently aquatic species.

Your cage size should be as large as you can make it. Although some states have guidelines that govern the minimum size of lizard cages (based on the number of lizards per cage and the total length of the largest lizard), these guidelines are adequate for species such as blue-tongued skinks and glass lizards. The guidelines are woefully inadequate for lizards that are as active as iguanas, monitors, and tegus.

In reality, an active lizard such as an iguana or monitor of six feet (1.83 m) or more in length, should be provided with an enclosure at least 8 feet × 10 feet (2.44 m × 3.05 m), with tree trunks and climbing limbs, elevated shelves, access to natural sunlight or a bank of UV-producing lights, a hotspot for basking, areas of seclusion, and an adequate supply of clean water.

Indeed, many keepers of large iguanas and/or monitors actually "donate" a spare room to their charge.

Caging for Smaller Lizards

Indoor cages for smaller lizards, or for babies of larger lizards, can be made of wire-covered wood framing, glass panels cut to size and glued together with silicone adhesive, or adapted from commercially available aquaria. Of course, any cage needs to have a lid that will close tightly.

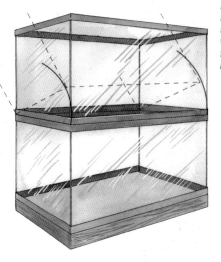

Commercial Aquaria

Standard aquaria can be easily adapted to different caging styles. They may be oriented horizontally or turned on the side for a vertical cage. If you opt for a vertical position, glue feet on the end of the tank that will serve as the bottom so that the clip-on screen top (which will then be a side) is easily put on and removed.

By removing the glass bottom of a second tank and placing it atop a second tank, you can create a terrarium of twice the height. Stacked tanks can be held in place with wide plastic tape along the back side. By sealing only the back, the top tank can be tilted back to create a center access. But handle these tanks carefully; once the bottom is completely removed, a glass tank loses much of its lateral rigidity and, thus, stability.

Making Your Own Custom Terrarium

Since the advent of silicon adhesive (Silastic aquarium sealant), making your own all-glass terrarium

To provide climbing space, well-secured stacked terraria or a cage on top of a glass terrarium may be designed.

Customized glass terraria of any size may be built indoors to accommodate lizards.

Although making a terrarium may sound simple, it is best to start by drawing a diagram of how you want the finished product to look. This is especially important if you are building one any more intricate than the standard rectangular shape. Accurate portrayal is important. You'll need to depict the size and shape of the bottom, top, sides (including the number), and door(s) (and where it/they are to be hung). Avoid the frustration of breaking glass as you cut it, and have a glazier cut the glass for you. By having all dimensions and numbers, the glazier can cut your glass quickly and entirely accurately. Use glass thick enough for your project. Do not underestimate the thickness needed. Have all edges smoothed at the time of cutting.

Once all materials are at hand, you can begin the construction phase. Although you can do this by yourself, you'll probably quickly realize that having a helper present will greatly ease things.

Caution: Before beginning construction, clean each pane of glass thoroughly. If fingerprints or cutting lubrication remain on the panes, the aquarium sealant will not properly adhere to the glass, resulting in structural weaknesses and perhaps breakage at a later date.

Assembly

The side panels, either three (corner tank), four (traditional tank), or more (hex tanks, etc.) should sit on top, *not on the outside,* of the bot-

is not an insurmountable task. In fact, besides the sealant and the accurately cut glass, the only absolute necessity will be a strong tape to hold your glass in place until the sealant sets. Hinges for most smaller doors can be made from a bead of the aquarium sealant, but larger doors will probably require actual hinges. The hinges can be held in place with aquarium sealant. Door latches can also be affixed with sealant.

tom panel. Place the bottom panel on a solid, flat surface and run a bead of sealant all the way around the outer edge of the upper surface. Set the first side panel atop the sealant, flush with the outer edge of the bottom. It is important that the side panels be perfectly vertical. Hold this panel in place (this is where the second person will come in very handy). Run a copious bead of sealant down one edge of the vertical panel and bring the next side panel into position. In this (and subsequent) case(s), you must have the panel sitting firmly atop the bead of sealant on the bottom panel, as well as firmly in contact with the sealant on the edge of the earlier placed side panel. Once two panels are in place, begin holding them there with strips of tape. Continue this procedure until all solid vertical panels (including partial panels on the side where your door will be, if applicable) are in place and are firmly in contact with each other. At this time, while the sealant is curing, be certain that all vertical panels are correctly positioned. Add more, or remove excess sealant as necessary and smooth the sealant along the inner surface of each joint with your finger (some persons prefer to wear disposable surgical gloves for this). Each inner joint should have a smoothly curved bead of sealant along the entire edge. The sealant should also be added, removed, and smoothed on the outer joints of all glass panels at this time. Air bubbles, if present in the sealant beads,

should be worked out. If left in place, air bubbles will significantly weaken the finished terrarium.

If you intend to use metal hinges held in place with aquarium sealant on your glass door, affix the hinges now.

After all unmovable panels are in place, allow a full 24 hours for the sealant to cure before continuing. At that time the top of the terrarium can be affixed and door panels can be positioned, held in place with tape, and the hinge affixed to the permanent terrarium glass with sealant. Small doors may not require an actual hinge. If small enough, the hinge may consist of just a large bead of Silastic. Remember, though, that a Silastic hinge will weaken with time and will need periodic renewing. The top may consist either partially or entirely of a glass panel, or may be of screen or welded wire with a wooden frame that has been mitered to exact size. Remember also that a terrarium made entirely of glass will have poor ventilation and will accumulate internal condensation. This situation may be desirable in an excessively dry climate, but is usually not desired.

Be sure no sharp edges are exposed anywhere on the tank. Should they remain, smooth them with emery cloth (taking care not to scratch the flat surfaces of the panel) and/or cover the rough area with a patina of sealant. Now, allow a minimum of another 24 hours for curing. Following that period, your tank is ready for use.

Shower Stalls

Easily moved and plumbed corner shower stalls are readily available in many home supply stores. These are usually constructed of a heavy molded plastic on two sides and have glass on the remaining two sides. If you have sufficient room and are looking for an excellent indoor cage for arboreal lizards, these stalls can be easily adapted to your purposes. All you need to add is a top and lighting.

Open-top Movable Plywood Cages

These low cages are ideal for lizard species such as blue-tongued and shingle-backed skinks, spiny-tailed agamids *(Uromastyx),* chuckwallas, desert iguanas, plated lizards, girdle-tailed lizards, and others with similar terrestrial or saxicolous lifestyles.

Materials necessary: 4 to 6 large casters
- a marine plywood bottom (sized as wanted)
- 4 sides of appropriate height, and an overhang for the 4 sides
- materials for a top (optional but suggested). The top serves as much to keep predators out as to keep the lizards in.

Suggestions: Properly affixed casters will allow you to easily move this cage. If you have an outside deck or porch, make the cage sufficiently narrow and low enough to allow it to be moved in or out through the door. Six feet or eight feet (1.83 m–2.44 m) long by two inches (5.1 cm) narrower and lower than your deck door will suffice. Sides of from 15 inches to 18 inches (38 cm–45.7 cm) are suggested. An overhang of from four inches to six inches (10.2 cm–15.2 cm) is usually sufficient.

The sides should be nailed (or screwed) in place atop the bottom panel; the overhang should be nailed in place atop the sides. The top, if provided, should fit tightly and be hinged on one side. A top that does not fit tightly will provide you with a false sense of security. It is probably better to have no top, rather than a poorly constructed one. When choosing a wire for the top, think anti-predator (dogs, cats, raccoons, crows, etc.), rather than lizard-holding. This is especially true if the cage is to be positioned on an open deck or porch.

Large Cages for Agile Lizards

Wood and Wire Cages

If you choose to make your own wood-framed cage, it is a small matter to build, hinge, and secure a top. If the top is separate from the cage, use clamps or place a brick atop each end to discourage unauthorized "wanderings." This may not be attractive, but it is functional. If the

cage is tall, the top should be affixed and the door built into the front. As your lizard(s) grows, it will require correspondingly more space.

A simple cage begins with a wooden framework. Then wire mesh is stapled to the outside of the framework. The bottom can be a piece of plywood (¾ inch [19 mm] is best, but ½ inch [12.7 m] will do) or can be wire mesh if the cage sits on a bed of newspaper. The supporting braces should be at least 2 × 2s.

Wire: The wire used can vary in strength and mesh size according to the type, size, and attitude of the lizard(s) you intend to house.

Welded wire mesh of at least ½-inch × ½-inch (12.7 mm) squares is suggested for large iguanas and monitors. A smaller mesh is apt to catch the toenails of these large lizards and could cause injury to the toes. If a smooth welded mesh or a plastic-covered wire is used, it will help prevent the lizard from abrading its nose if it tries to escape.

A smaller mesh can be used if the cage is intended to house smaller lizard species such as geckos, water dragons, anoles, basilisks, etc. Since it prevents the escape of all but the smallest crickets (an important consideration with insect-eating lizards), we use ⅛-inch (3.2 mm) welded mesh.

Do not use plastic screening. It is too easily ripped and crickets will quickly chew their way through the screen.

Position your wood and wire cage to make the best use of existing weather conditions. Having casters on the cage bottom will allow ease of movement.

the desired shape and then joined. This works best if the wire used is of relatively heavy gauge, welded, and has openings ½ inch × 1 inch (12.7 mm × 25 mm) in size.

We have found the precut panels (or those we have cut ourself) easiest to work with. They are easily joined with little flat metal brads called "J-clamps" that are crimped with a special tool and are sold specifically for the purpose of wire joining. The wire, the J-clamps, and pliers are sold in hardware and feed stores.

An advantage of all-wire cages is that they are lighter than those framed of wood. Because the mesh used is welded, the cages are quite stable. We have made permanent (unmovable) cages up to eight feet long × three feet wide and six feet high (2.4 m × .91 m × 1.83 m) in this manner. These have proven ideal for tame lizards that don't mind being approached, as well as for naturally quiet species. Among others, we have kept green and ground iguanas, prehensile-tailed skinks, and tame water monitors in these arrangements.

Smaller all-wire mesh cages are strong enough to be easily moved. If this is your intent, we suggest that you consider a maximum size of six feet × three feet × four feet (1.83 m × .91 m × 1.22 m).

Some lizards will persistently abrade their noses in cages of this style, especially in the movable ones that, in an effort to keep them light, often do not contain criss-

The braces can be nailed or screwed together and the mesh stapled in place. When housing lizards as strong as adult iguanas and monitors, hammer-in wire staples (rather than those from a small staple gun) are suggested. Be sure the door is large enough for you to reach the bottom of the cage, to clean it, or add another door near the bottom of the cage for this purpose.

All-wire Mesh Cages

Cages for large lizards can be easily made from precut welded wire panels or the mesh may be bent into

crosses of limbs and other visual barriers. Initially watch any lizards that you place in these cages to be sure that they are not injuring themselves. If they are, remove them to more suitable quarters.

Glass-fronted Plywood Cages

If you prefer a heavier cage, you can build one from plywood sheeting with wood-framed glass doors. The plywood cage will require sizable screened ventilation panels on each end. If wire is used in the ventilation panels, make certain it is welded and the mesh is large enough to avoid injury. Due to its size and lack of ventilation, this sort of caging is for indoor use only.

Aluminum Rings

We were very successful in breeding several species of lacertid lizards, small monitors, and large skinks in outside, quasi-natural facilities, in southwest Florida.

The cages were circular, eight feet to ten feet (2.44 m–3.05 m) diameter, simple, and relatively inexpensive.

The walls were made from three-foot-high (.91 m) aluminum sheeting sunk one foot (.30 m) into the ground. We found that the easiest way to outline and sink the sheeting was to use a posthole digger attached to a 4.5 foot (1.37 m) length of twine. The other end of the twine was noosed loosely around a post tapped into the ground where the center of the cage was to be. By keeping the posthole digger at the

outer limit of the twine, it was a relatively simple matter to dig the foot-deep trench needed for the aluminum. No footer was needed. The aluminum sheeting was then set into the trench, leveled (this can be painstaking), and the two ends riveted together. The trench was then filled on both sides, with particular care given to the inside perimeter. Once the filling of the trench was complete, the cage was essentially finished. The small diameter terra cotta drainage pipes were then buried, pyramids of stones placed strategically, water supplied, and the lizards introduced. In our area (Lee County, Florida), these cages worked well and, since predators were not common, required no tops. Where either or both winged and four-footed predators (hawks, crows, cats, raccoons, opossums) are common, a top must be made for these otherwise open-air cages. The top can be framed from 1 × 2s

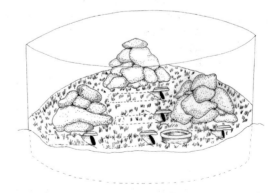

A ring of aluminum, sunk a foot (.3 m) into the ground, makes an escape-proof outdoor cage for many small-to medium-sized lizard species.

Many lizards, such as this shield-tailed agama, will be most comfortable when provided with hideboxes or a substrate into which they can burrow.

and covered with ¼-inch (6.4 mm) mesh hardware cloth, or you could sink a center stake and drape bird netting over the entire cage.

Plastic Storage Boxes

Over the years, American herpetoculturists have become known for caging reptiles and amphibians in the simplest, most utilitarian manner possible. American hobbyists often opt for little more than an absorbent bottom of folded newspaper, paper towels or aspen shavings, an untippable water bowl, and a hidebox. Believe it or not, this type of caging works for leopard, fat-tailed, and other terrestrial geckos. Not only do they live well in such simple vivaria, but most will breed prolifically.

Plastic shoe, sweater, and blanket boxes are available in many hardware and department stores. Be sure the lids fit securely, or can be secured with tape or velcro strips. Add plenty of ventilation holes by drilling or melt-ing a series of holes through at least two sides, and all four is better.

Cabinets that hold a dozen or more plastic boxes are now available, many with heat tapes built in. These are advertised in most reptile magazines and at many of the reptile meets.

"European-Style" Caging

In direct contrast to the starkness preferred by most American hobbyists, their European counterparts have become well known for the intricacy of detail that goes into the construction of their terrarium interiors. The Europeans, it seems, prefer to reconstruct a little corner of nature, a working, miniaturized ecosystem, in their terraria. This concept has stood the Europeans in good stead, for many of the lizards still considered difficult to breed by American hobbyists, are routinely produced in impressive numbers in Europe.

To successfully create a terrarium of the European style takes knowledge, time, and dedication. To succeed with it you need not only an understanding of the lizard inhabitants, but an understanding of the dynamics of their habitat as well. Although the more natural setting is more conducive to normal behavior by the lizards, it is actually far more difficult to maintain suitable conditions in a European-style setup than in one of the more Spartan American cages. The desert, woodland, and semiaquatic terraria described herein are actually of simplified European design.

Cage Furniture

In nature, most lizards have a home turf—a burrow, or crevice, or hollow trunk to which they regularly return after foraging and at night. They are more secure in captivity when this provision is made.

Safe, functional, and properly placed cage furniture is important to the well-being of your lizards. As with all other aspects of lizard husbandry, you should consider the normal habits of the species you are keeping when designing cages.

For instance, the little corytophanid lizard, *Corytophanes cristata* (often sold as "forest iguana" or "forest chameleon"), prefers to cling tightly to vertical, or nearly vertical, trunks of fair diameter. Many arboreal geckos (including leaf-tails of the genus *Uroplatus*) also prefer such vertical vantage points. The corytophanid cone-headed lizards (genus *Laemanctus*) and many of the smaller arboreal anoles are entirely at home amidst the treetop foliage. Some lizard species change their vantage points seasonally. Both vertical perches and a leafy canopy should be provided.

Hideboxes

Small terrestrial lizards, such as desert night lizards, leopard and fat-tailed geckos, smaller skinks, many lacertids, and others with similar lifestyles, will readily accept hollowed and bleached cholla (*Opuntia*) cactus skeletons, rock or plastic caves, or even inverted flowerpot saucers (with access holes added), as hiding areas. While certainly a natural appearing hidebox, the cholla may prove *too* secure for the preferences of many keepers. Once the lizards are inside, it is usually difficult to induce them to leave without poking or prodding, both of which should be discouraged. Cholla skeletons are also ideal hiding places for the eggs and young of ectoparasites such as mites, making them difficult to eradicate. Avoid cedar hideboxes— the phenols in that wood are harmful to all reptiles.

Unless they are firmly affixed, or have baffles affixed to them, rocks can shift position when lizards burrow beneath and may injure, or actually crush, the specimens they were intended to aid.

We have found flowerpot saucers ideal. If plastic, an access can be easily cut with shears or tinsnips; if clay, the access can be gently and carefully nipped out with a pair of needle-nosed pliers.

Diurnal lizards need both bright lighting and a warm cage for normal behavior.

Arboreal lizards, such as this young veiled chameleon, Chamaeleo calyptratus, *will require leafy boughs or sturdy potted plants in their cage.*

Textured and contoured plastic hideboxes are available commercially. Some are simply hideboxes, others incorporate a watering dish into their design.

For larger terrestrial lizards such as tegus, monitors, iguanas, blue-tongued skinks, etc., hideboxes can be made from inverted cat litter trays, plastic dishpans, or opaque plastic storage boxes, all with an entry hole cutout.

Although a custom box can be provided, even a simple closed cardboard box with an entrance hole provides security for your lizard.

In all cases, when space permits, we actually prefer two hideboxes, one on the warm end and one on the cool side of the tank.

Arboreal lizards (prehensile-tailed skinks, emerald and black monitors, green iguanas, etc.) will enjoy a hid-ing area affixed near the top of their cage. We usually offer hollowed logs wired or bracketed securely in place, but commercially available hides such as cockatiel or parrot nesting boxes (with entry holes enlarged as necessary) are also well accepted by most lizards.

Corkbark

Tubes of corkbark are readily available and impart a naturalistic effect to terraria. If wedged securely, lizards can not only bask on the upper surface, but the inside of the tubes provide a wonderfully secluded area that most arboreal lizards readily use. The sculptured outer surface of the corkbark is an ideal holdtight for epiphytic bromeli-ads, orchids, and ferns, all plant types that are favored by terrarium keepers.

Outside Cages

For our terrestrial lizards that are caged outside, we provide hollowed limbs resting securely on the ground, rock piles, and a labyrinth of buried clay pipes (which double in the winter as hibernacula) for terrestrial forms.

Limbs

With heat lamps correctly positioned, limbs and even sizable trunks (or flat shelves) are enjoyed by lizards both as basking areas and as vantage points. Except for the canopy dwellers, which are at home in the comparative instability of treetop leaves and breeze-buffeted twigs, most lizards prefer a basking limb of at least the diameter of their body, and are even more at home on one that is about one and a half times their body diameter. Most lizards prefer limbs positioned horizontally or weakly sloping but, as mentioned earlier, others will prefer vertical trunks. Research the natural history of your lizards and provide them with their normal preferences. If you are unable to find references to the natural history of your lizard species, opt for diversity in limb positioning.

Limbs cut to the exact inside length of glass terraria can be secured at any desired level with thick U-shaped beads of silicone aquarium sealant that have been placed on the cleaned aquarium glass. Once the sealant is dry, merely slide the limb downward through the open top until it rests securely on the bottom of the U.

Foliage

Because dedicated greenery (forest plants for woodland terraria, dry-adapted plants for aridland terraria, etc.) so effectively affords visual barriers and a feeling of security, where possible we incorporate plantings into our cages. We have found potted *Ficus benjamina* ideally adaptable to moderate to high light situations both indoors and outdoors, and *F. benjamina* can even be temporarily used in low light situations. The dragon plants of the genus *Dracaena* are also excellent choices for most moderate to high light setups. Although tolerant of low light conditions, these plants will eventually deteriorate. Neither the *Ficus* nor the *Dracaena* like perpetually wet roots.

Succulents and cacti of many species and cultivars are readily available from nurseries. In high light, low moisture situations, these interesting plants will thrive, producing wonderfully colored blooms from time to time.

Hanging pots of *Syngonium, Epipremnum (=Pothos), Philodendron,* and ivy can be used in tall terraria and cages. Lizards such as basilisks and water dragons will often dig their nests in the easier to reach pots that, if kept suitably moist and warm, make ideal incubators.

Some day geckos (genus *Phelsuma)* habitually lay their eggs in tubular growing plants such as the sturdy sanseverias (also referred to as "snake plants" or "mother-in-law-tongues") and the hardier bromeliad species are always an appropriate consideration for terraria containing smaller arboreal lizards (geckos, anoles, coneheads, etc.). Small, hardy epiphytic orchids and ferns are also often grown in terraria. Although many of these are somewhat more tender than bromeliads, together they provide an appearance of tropical lushness. Despite the fact that many of these plants grow in reduced light situations in the wild, when in terraria most actually do best in rather strong artificial light and when relative humidity is kept high.

Rock Formations

Many of the spiny lizards, collared lizards, geckos, and agamas are at home on escarpments and amid cliffside exfoliations. These, and other species, will readily use rock formations of varying heights for both vantage points and seclusion.

Spiny lizards, geckos, agamas, and other such cliff-face lizards will enjoy stacked rock formations with fissures into which they can dart and hide.

Collared lizards and other predatory species that use rocks as a vantage point from which an ambush can be effected, will happily use a single large rock projecting well above the substrate.

In all cases, the rock formations should begin right against the bottom glass of the terrarium. By doing this, your lizards will be unable to burrow beneath and shift the forma-

tion. Silicone adhesive works well for holding rock formations securely together. As with limbs, a heat lamp can be positioned above the rock, which will then become the most desirable station in the terrarium.

Substrate

The floor covering of your indoor cage can consist of any number of items. We feel that newspaper or wrapping paper is ideal in many cases. Astroturf and indoor/outdoor carpeting will work but is hard to keep clean and free from bacterial and protozoan buildup. We have used cypress or aspen shavings (never cedar) and mulch very successfully. Both are readily available, nontoxic, and inexpensive. Dried leaves are easily available and are pleasing to the eye. Even rabbit food (compressed alfalfa pellets) can be used but, like carpeting, tends to hold moisture and must be changed frequently. In a room-sized cage (or the room itself), a linoleum or tile covering is often used. This is easily mopped and disinfected when soiled.

A lizard may repeatedly defecate in a particular area of its cage. This may be in the water dish (which must then be cleaned and sterilized immediately) or in a provided receptacle as small as a margarine dish (for geckos) or as large as a kitty pan for iguanas or monitors. In either case, the receptacle should contain a little sand, which then makes the cleaning of the pan a simple matter.

Most diurnal lizards will require strong illumination and warmed basking areas. This small desert terrarium has a UV-producing light (left) and a basking light (right).

Lighting and Heating

The lifestyles of lizards vary tremendously by species. The variables include both lighting and heating preferences. Lizards may be arboreal heliotherms (sun baskers), terrestrial heliotherms, terrestrial or saxicolous thigmotherms (species that absorb heat from the substrate, often while in seclusion or during nocturnal activities), or combinations of all of these and still other lifestyles. Lizards dwell in the intense heat of the deserts, in the relative chill of montane meadows, in the tropics, and in temperate regions.

As might be imagined, both lighting and heat availability vary as greatly as the lifestyles of the lizards. Light and warmth are mandatory for the long-term well-being of your heliothermic lizards. It is at a body temperature of 88 to 95°F (31–35°C) that your many heliotherms are most active and disease-resistant. Certain desert-dwelling heliothermic lizards may preferentially attain even higher body temperatures. Indeed, some desert forms may thermoregulate in open, heat-reflecting sand until their body temperature exceeds 100°F (37.8°C) and be able to tolerate at least ten degrees more before reaching a lethal maximum. Others, dwellers of the lower boles of rainforest trees, may be adapted to ambient temperatures of 78 to 85°F (25.6–29°C) and seldom, if

selves lengthwise along a sturdy limb, drooping their legs and part of their tails over the sides. In the wild, such basking stations are often above waterways into which the lizards may drop if startled. Rock-dwelling species often bask in the sunlight in front of a deep fissure or crevice into which they can dart if disturbed. Terrestrial aridland dwellers are often encountered in or near concealing patches of shrubby vegetation.

While you won't be able to provide the waterway, cliff-face rock exfoliations, or desert shrubs for your lizards, you can provide the sun-warmed limb or a sandy area on which to sprawl. A limb with bark will be much easier for your lizard to climb and cling to than one that has been peeled.

An elevated basking branch that is *at least* the diameter of the lizard's body, will be readily used by most species. If the limb is elevated only slightly above floor level, even normally terrestrial species may utilize it extensively. If more than one lizard is present, more than one basking platform should be provided, each illuminated and warmed. The limb(s) must be securely affixed to prevent toppling.

Direct the warming beams of one or two floodlight bulbs onto this perch from above. A temperature of 95 to 105°F (35–40.6°C) (measured on the top of the basking limb) should be created. Be certain to position the bulbs so your lizard(s) cannot burn itself if

ever, bask. Some montane species may attain peak activity with body temperatures in the high 60s°F (18.9–20.6°C), low 70s°F (21–23°C), or even lower. The keyword here is diversity. Assume nothing. Research, and be sure you are able to provide for the needs of the lizard species in which you are interested *before* you acquire it. And don't stop at temperature and lighting; research the necessary relative humidity as well. Only when at their optimum will your lizards be basically stress-free and able to successfully approach and overcome any and all exigencies.

Duplicating a Sunlit Habitat

Whether kept indoors or out, your diurnal lizards will require adequate heat and light. You will need to duplicate a sunlit habitat within their cage or room. Many lizards, and especially iguanas and monitors, like to sprawl while basking. Arboreal species will position them-

it approaches the lamp. Currently, we use large, incandescent plant-growth bulbs for this purpose; however, "full-spectrum" incandescent bulbs have recently appeared in the pet market. To date, since UV rays are not emitted, these bulbs would be better termed "color-corrected" than "full-spectrum." Hopefully improvements will be made.

Full-spectrum Lighting

Is full-spectrum (UV-emitting) lighting actually necessary to the well-being of your monitor or tegu? Well, perhaps not absolutely necessary, but the UV-A and UV-B emissions are beneficial, even in only small amounts.

UV-A helps promote natural behavior in reptiles (see cautions in handling, pages 50–53) and UV-B controls the synthesis of vitamin D_3 in the reptile's skin. When natural synthesis occurs, it allows for greater error in feeding supplements.

Let's look at this in a little more detail.

In all truthfulness, when it comes to assessing the true benefits of artificial UV emissions, the jury is still out. Many keepers of heliothermic lizards consider the use of full-spectrum lighting mandatory; others, however, have kept and bred various lizard species without ever using full-spectrum lighting. We are ambivalent on the subject, but have never considered *not* using full-spectrum lighting.

Lizards that are provided with full-spectrum lighting, especially UV-A,

do seem to display more normal behavior than those that are not so provided. And since normalcy of specimens is what most of us involved in herpetoculture are striving for, we always suggest that full-spectrum lighting be used. There are now many brands of UV-producing bulbs—both incandescent and fluorescent—available. Check the output of all available and choose the one that emits the most UV. It is UV-A and UV-B rays that you are hoping to provide your lizard with. Even when a bulb is new, the amount of these rays emitted is low. To gain any advantage from the bulb, your lizard must be able to bask within 6 inches to 12 inches (13 m–30.5 cm) of it. Typical of any fluorescent tube, Vita-Lite bulbs give off little heat but a wire baffle of some sort should prevent the lizard from coming less than six inches (13 cm) from the bulb.

Only cages of wood and wire construction should be placed outdoors. In hope of an easy meal of food insects, wild lizards often are drawn to these cages.

Position the fixture and baffles accordingly.

Although the true benefits to your lizard from artificial lighting sources is conjectural, the benefit from one lighting source is not—and this source is as close as your back door.

Natural Sunlight

Natural, unfiltered sunlight unquestionably provides the best possible lighting (and heat) for any heliothermic lizard. You may have been wondering why we earlier stressed that your cages should always be able to pass through your doorways and be on casters. Here is why: It will allow you to move your lizards—still securely caged—outdoors on warm, sunny days. In most cases the casters will allow one person to accomplish this otherwise unwieldy task. There is simply nothing better that you can do for your lizards.

CAUTION: Only cages constructed of wood and wire should be placed out in the sun and even they should be watched closely until the temperatures attained within are truly determined. A glass terrarium not only filters out the UV, but a glass terrarium, even with a screen top, or none, will intensify and accumulate heat. This can literally cook your lizards in just a few minutes, even on a relatively cool day! Be sure to provide a shaded area for your lizard even in the wood/wire cages.

If you live in an area where it is absolutely impossible to get your lizard outside, perhaps you could allow it to bask in an opened window on hot summer days. Natural, unfiltered sunlight from any vantage point will be beneficial.

Window Cages: To make this possible for more hobbyists, a window cage that slides in and out of an opened window on extendible tracks has been developed. This should prove a real boon to apartment, condo, or city dwellers who would be otherwise unable to allow their lizards access to natural sunlight.

Rather than purchasing a window cage, you may choose to build your lizard a less sophisticated, but suitably sized cage of wood and wire, or of wire panels J-clamped together. This can be hooked or wedged into a window and, although less convenient than a cage on tracks, will more than suffice and be considerably cheaper.

In all cases, do remember the earlier admonitions regarding excessive heat buildup. Carefully monitor the high temperatures in the cage at all times and provide a shaded area to which your lizards can retreat if they choose.

Altering Humidity

Proper cage humidity is an important but often overlooked aspect of herpetoculture. If you are keeping desert species and the humidity is too high, the lizards will decline in health. If you are keeping rainforest lizards and the humidity is too low, shedding and other health-related problems will result.

Cage humidity can be altered by changing the size of the water dish

An albino fat-tailed gecko, Hemitheconyx caudicinctus, *prowls through his naturalistically decorated terrarium.*

or by increasing or decreasing the amount of ventilation. Screen tops or sides allow ventilation. To increase ventilation provide more open screening; to reduce ventilation, provide less screening.

Cage humidity can be raised by growing plants in the terrarium. When trying to maintain a low humidity (such as in a desert terrarium), plant types that need little water (cacti and succulents) should be used. In the case of a rainforest terrarium, where high relative humidity is the aim, moisture-loving vining plants such as *Epipremnum* (pothos) and philodendrons can be used.

Artificial plants can also be used to advantage. Some artificial plants are said to exude harmful vapors for years after being manufactured so ascertain that those you use do not. The advantage of artificial plants is that, since they need no moisture, they will not increase cage humidity at all. Also, they are easily washed when soiled, can be placed exactly where you wish them to be, and require virtually no care at all.

In our eyes, however, artificial plants provide none of the beauty and naturalness of living plants. We consider the former to be a poor second choice, at best.

Chapter Three
Watering Techniques

Not all lizards need water dishes continually in place. This is especially true of arboreal species that are misted daily and desert species that are adapted to metabolize most of their water needs from their food. As a matter of fact, for the latter, a water dish (which raises cage humidity) can be harmful. We suggest that you research the lifestyle of the species you are keeping and tailor the water availability, and the method in which it is supplied, accordingly.

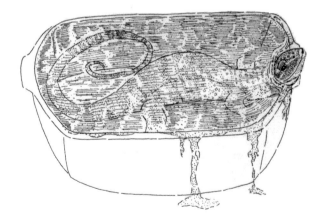

Semi-aquatic lizards such as monitors soak in their watering dish.

Water Dishes and Humidity

As mentioned above, the presence or lack of water in a cage coupled with the amount of cage ventilation can dramatically alter cage humidity. The larger the surface of the water dish and the more restricted the cage ventilation, the higher the cage humidity. Cage humidity can be raised almost to saturation by placing a heating unit under the water bowl. While such humidity may be fine for rainforest or riverine lizard species, it will be quickly fatal to dwellers of dry deserts. To reduce humidity, do not use a heating pad under the water bowl—use a smaller water receptacle and increase cage ventilation. In normally humid areas (the southeastern coastal plain, fog belts, the Pacific Northwest), even with water bowls entirely removed, it may be difficult to reduce cage humidity enough to successfully keep some desert reptile species without the use of a dehumidifier in the room. When water bowls are removed, you must take care that your lizards remain sufficiently hydrated. To ensure this, if the lizards are of a normally "tame" species (chuckwallas, collared lizards, bearded dragons), water may be given daily with an eyedropper or pipette, or you can move the lizards to a cage where they can be watered normally, once or twice a week, or as necessary.

Cleanliness: When a water receptacle is provided, it must be kept scrupulously clean. Regular sterilization will help prevent the transmission of endoparasites. For lizards that regularly soak, the water must also be kept suitably warm to avoid respiratory problems. The possibility of respiratory problems increases when low humidity air moves freely through the cage causing evaporative cooling.

Soaking: Many lizards, especially semiaquatic ones, will regularly bask and stool in their water supply. They seem most prone to do so almost immediately after you have painstakingly cleaned and replaced the water receptacle, leaving you no recourse but to reclean and refill the container.

If given a large enough container of tepid water, many lizards will soak for long periods. Among these inveterate soakers are water and Nile monitors, water dragons, basilisks, frilled lizards, and tegus.

Adult Nile and water monitors, which may exceed a heavy-bodied seven feet (2.13 m) in length, may require a soaking container nearly the size of a bathtub. It is best, and will certainly be easiest for you, if you have the tub plumbed into your waste water disposal system. At the very least, a drain should be installed in the floor of the tub, and perhaps in the floor of the room, to help you with what might very well be a daily (or twice daily) cleaning project.

Normal drinking: Many lizards do not prefer to soak, but do need to be able to drink daily. For these forms a small, shallow drinking receptacle will suffice. As it is for the soaking water, it is important that drinking water be kept absolutely clean.

Watering Arboreal Lizards

Arboreal lizards may not readily descend to the ground to drink from a pan. This is especially true of disoriented, newly imported lizards that, until capture, probably derived

A drip bucket is an effective way to water arboreal lizards.

A good misting falls like a gentle rain.

placed in an easily accessible area and at a level where the lizards feel comfortable.

Misting

This is, of course, an excellent watering technique. Indoors this can be done with a spray bottle; outside with a misting nozzle. In either case, do not spray the lizards directly. Rather, direct the spray upwards and let the droplets fall like rain.

most (if not all) of their water requirements from water-filled treeholes and from lapping water flowing down limbs, trunks, and foliage during storms. For these lizards it is best to place a water receptacle on an elevated shelf near a favored basking or resting area. We have found that some chameleons, most anoles, both the emerald and black tree monitors, and many other species, will readily drink from a water dish placed in the pot of an easily accessible hanging plant. They seem to notice, and be drawn to the plant by the fresh droplets of water that remain on the leaves following mistings. It is very important that you place all water dishes where even the most seclusive of your lizards will readily notice and drink from them.

Arboreal lizards will also usually be drawn to a dish of water that has the surface roiled by an aquarium air stone. Again, the dish should be

Hydration Chambers

Hydration chambers have long been used by zoos and other institutions and are coming into general use by private herpetoculturists and hobbyists. Hydration chambers are actually rain chambers, and these devices can make the difference between life and death for dehydrated rainforest and humid woodland lizards. The chambers also serve a vital function in the reproductive cycling of these and other reptiles and amphibians.

Making Your Own

An open hydration chamber can be constructed of wire mesh over a wood frame. A closed system can be made from an aquarium equipped with a circulating water pump and a screen or perforated plexiglass top. If you live in a benign climate where the wood and

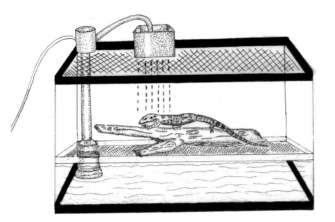

A hydration chamber helps restore a lizard's hydration level.

wire cage can be placed outdoors, a mist nozzle can be placed on the end of a hose, affixed over the cage, and fresh water run through this for an hour or more a day.

If indoors, the wood and wire cage can be placed on top, or inside a properly drained utility tub, and tap water used.

In closed systems, the circulation pump moves water from the bottom of the tank to the tank top, and the water then drips down through a perforated PVC pipe or drips through the screen top over the tank. It is imperative that the water in self-contained systems be kept immaculate.

Why Use a Chamber?

These units can help moisture-deprived reptiles and amphibians recuperate. Those that will most benefit are the rainforest species that are freighted long distances to reach the pet markets of America, Asia, Europe, and other areas. Among other lizards, the various anoles, chameleons, water dragons, basilisks, tree monitors, and some geckos are often helped by the use of these chambers. Use for an hour a day for several days to treat dehydrated lizards. Desert species will need fewer days; forest species may need more.

Chapter Four
Understanding Diets

What happens when a normally herbivorous lizard is fed excessive animal protein (including insects), or when an insect-eating lizard is fed a diet heavy on, or exclusively of, pinky mice?

The truth is, we don't really know! Available diets seem to influence the well-being of lizards differently under different conditions.

For example, while a free iguana seems to be able to eat a moderate quantity of animal protein with no ill effects, when that same diet is provided to a captive, gout and other such diseases eventually occur. Perhaps, in the wild, the natural feeding, watering, levels of UV lighting, or greater activity level of the lizard, singly or in combination, forestall problems. Or perhaps the lizard benefits from chemicals contained in readily available food leaves. Whatever the reason, wild iguanas can, and do, eat differently than captives and seem not to develop particular problems. Nor are they the only lizards to do so.

Despite the fact that we want to do what is best for our captive lizards, it is human nature to seek the easiest method of completing any task. If the pathway chosen merely means that you build a week's supply of salad for your lizard at one time, thus reducing your daily workload, no harm can come from your efforts. But if in lightening your workload you incorporate more readily available animal protein into your lizard's diet, the long-term use will probably result in the onset of one or more diet-related diseases.

The use of such readily available items as low-fat dog food, monkey chow, mice, crickets, mealworms,

A "reptilian cow," the green iguana, Iguana iguana, *is entirely herbivorous.*

and other sources of animal protein in the diet of an herbivorous lizard (iguana, prehensile-tailed skink, etc.) is contraindicated. This may be especially difficult for the new lizard keeper to understand, for all of these items were once considered to be beneficial for most lizards and may still be suggested by the personnel of some pet shops.

Pinky Mice

We come to another gray area when the feeding of pinky mice to insectivorous lizards is considered. Pinkies, smaller than some of the insects eaten regularly by many insectivorous lizards, contain a far higher fat content than insects. When used in moderation, pinkies probably cause no problem, but, when used exclusively, as is often the case, obesity, visceral problems, and, most recently, seemingly irreversible corneal lipid buildups, are being encountered in our pet lizards.

Although normally insectivorous lizards seem to thrive for long periods—sometimes years—on a diet of pinkies, a diet varied in content seems infinitely better.

Not unsurprisingly, studies, some long-term, but all probably still preliminary, correlate good lizard health with good lizard diet, and indicate that what constitutes a good diet in the wild is not necessarily similar to what should be offered in captivity. Other studies have indicated that certain lizard species are more tolerant of our dietary shortcuts than others. We will mention some particulars in the various species accounts beginning on page 64.

Diets for Herbivorous Lizards

Frequently seen examples of herbivorous lizards are:
- Prehensile-tailed skink, *Corucia zebrata*
- Green Iguanas, *Iguana iguana*
- All other iguanas, genera *Ctenosaura, Cyclura, Dipsosaurus,* etc.
- Chuckwallas, genus *Sauromalus*
- Spiny-tailed agamids, *Uromastyx*

Although this might sound like a simple way to define a category of lizards, determining exactly which plants a lizard of any species con-

An iguana food pyramid—heavy on vegetables and fruit, very light on animal protein.

sumes, from babyhood through old age, is not an easy task. The non-natural effects of artificial lighting must be considered a part of the nutrition equation, and the type and amount of vitamin/mineral additives to be used must be determined. In the wild, optimum metabolic rates, unfettered movement, the very best of full-spectrum lighting (the sun!), natural foods, water supply, and humidity undoubtedly stand the creatures in good stead. There, most herbivorous lizards (especially babies) will opportunistically eat succulent insects or other animal matter (perhaps carrion). This tendency is carried over by most lizards to captive conditions, where most kinds of herbivorous lizards will eagerly accept animal protein when offered.

A lapse from the proper diet seems to matter more to lizards in the artificial (stressful) confines we provide than to those in the wild. Thus, herbivorous lizards that are continually offered, and that frequently consume, animal protein, whether insects, pinky mice, moistened or rehydrated dog or cat foods, monkey chow, or other such materials, will often develop visceral gout, joint debilities, metabolic bone disease, soft tissue mineralization, or other such diet-related maladies, at some point in their life.

Keep in mind that reptiles do nothing quickly except to dart from danger. It may be months or even years after the incorrect diet has begun before external signs are manifested. Sadly, once the external manifestations are apparent, it is often either impossible, or at least very difficult, to reverse the progression of the problem(s).

Solutions to Bad Diets

As with all other animals, the best medicine is prevention, and if you err at all in husbandry, do so on the side of conservatism. Research the species in question in the scientific literature and/or in the very newest of the captive care manuals/handbooks. (Often, the scientific literature will advise you of the stomach contents of sacrificed specimens. It is not likely that you will be able to duplicate the kinds of plants eaten, but you can learn what percentage of the stomach contents was vegetable matter and what percentage was animal.) The information in the literature may conflict strongly with that given to you by some pet store employees. Should this be so, we strongly urge that you defer to the suggestions in the book.

Recommended Foods

Provide your pet herbivorous lizard a varied diet, while remembering that, as far as food values go, not all vegetables are created equal. Some vegetables, such as iceberg (sandwich) lettuce, have almost no food value at all. When using leafy vegetables choose those that are the darkest. Romaine, escarole, kale, turnip greens, collards, mustard greens, dandelion greens and flowers, bok choy, and nasturtiums (all parts) are all excellent foods. Rose and hibiscus blossoms are also appreciated, as are unsweetened bran cereals, alfalfa pellets and sprouts, clover leaves and blossoms, beans (including leaves and stems), grated squash, apples, various hays and grasses, and grain breads. Tofu and other soybean products are fine foods and enjoyed by many herbivorous lizards.

The variety of plant materials consumed is amazing. Spiny-tailed agamids (*Uromastyx* sp.) enjoy both fresh and dried legumes, a mixture of wild bird seeds, and small amounts of moistened chick-starter mash in their diets.

Calcium/D_3 supplements are probably very beneficial to most herbivorous reptiles, especially those that do not have access to natural, unfiltered sunlight.

Many basically herbivorous lizards, iguanas, spiny-tailed agamids (*Uromastyx* sp.), and chuckwallas among them, will become addicted to insects and rehydrated animal-protein chows. It is the feeling of many keepers that if the lizards like these food items, then the food items must be good for them. This train of thought equates with us living on a diet of banana splits because we like them. It just won't work.

Get your lizard—your iguana, your spiny-tailed agamid, or whatever—on a correct diet as quickly as possible, and keep it on that diet.

Dandelion blossoms and leaves are good food for herbivorous lizards.

Correcting Your Lizard's Diet

There are times when you may acquire a lizard that has long been maintained on an incorrect diet. Since it may take months, or even years, for the effects of an improper diet to be reflected in declining health, your new lizard may appear entirely normal in all respects. However, be assured that if over time the diet remains incorrect, your animal's health will eventually be seriously compromised. The diet must be corrected.

In the ideal scenario, your lizard would simply begin to eat the new diet when you presented it; however, that is seldom the case, especially if the lizard has eaten a specific item over a long period. It may then be necessary to resort to subterfuge or downright starvation to effect the necessary diet change. Begin, of course, by mixing the new dietary components with the old. It may be necessary to finely dice everything and mix thoroughly, but sometimes

Safe Foods for Lizards

Alfalfa
Apple
Avocado
Berries (straw, blue, elder, etc.)
Bok Choy
Broccoli stems and leaves
Cabbage (dark green or red, not
  white)
Dandelions
Escarole
Grated root crops (carrots,
  beets, etc.)
Grated squash
Greens (turnip, collard, mustard,
  beet)
Hibiscus blooms and leaves
Leaf lettuces (dark types)
Melons
Nasturtium
Okra
Papaya
Peaches
Pear
Romaine
Rose petals
Tofu
Tomato

this works. If your lizard refuses the new diet, don't worry—yet. Present it daily. If your lizard continues to pick out only its favored items, a finer puree may make this selection impossible. Lizards will also be more apt to accept a change in diet if they are hungry—in some cases, extremely hungry. To add this increment to a food change, merely withhold all food for a day or several days, keeping in mind the size and condition of your lizard. Continue to provide water for your lizard in the normal fashion during this changeover. You want it to be hungry, not dehydrated.

Toxic Plants Versus Safe Food

Many lists of so-called toxic plants have been compiled, but keep in mind that what is toxic to humans may not be toxic to animals. Poison ivy berries and mushrooms known to be poisonous to humans are eaten with impunity by many creatures. So, too, are many of the more toxic fruits of solanaceous plants (nightshades). What is poisonous to one group of animals may be a delicacy to others. In the wild, reptiles probably recognize naturally occurring, potentially problematic plants by odor or by the slightest taste.

Listed opposite are some plants that are known to be safe foods for your lizard. Besides those listed, there are many other safe and nutritious plants. Please remember that inclusion in this list has no bearing whatever on food value. It merely means that this plant is a nontoxic (safe) food for your lizard (or other herbivorous reptile).

Spinach and Swiss chard are not toxic but act as calcium binders, meaning that they inhibit the lizard's ability to absorb calcium from its diet. If you use spinach as a food item, be sure to increase the supplementary calcium. We do not offer spinach because there are so many other plant foods available that do not pose this problem.

A note about vegetables that contain a high percentage of available phosphorus and/or oxalic acid: The diet of any herbivorous lizard should provide a much higher percentage of calcium than phosphorus, and include few, if any, plants that would inhibit calcium metabolization. Typical examples of calcium binders are spinach and wood sorrel. The minimum ratio of calcium to phosphorus would be 2:1; 3:1 or 4:1 would be better. To find out the calcium:phosphorous content of a food plant, consult publications such as the "Composition of Foods, Handbook Number 8," published by the USDA in 1983.

Diets for Insectivorous Lizards

Frequently seen examples of insectivorous lizards include:
- True chameleons
- Brown and green anoles
- Most skink species
- Night lizards
- Most geckos
- Alligator lizards
- Glass lizards

Of the several feeding categories, diets for insectivorous lizards are the easiest to formulate. The name says it all—or almost all.

As you would surmise, insectivorous lizards eat insects, or at least

Crickets, grasshoppers, mealworms, small moths, and other insects are typical fare for insectivorous lizards.

primarily insects. Some species (collared and leopard lizards) are predacious and will not only eat insects, but will eat smaller lizards and pinky mice as well. We have had several collared lizards eat an occasional dandelion blossom. Some of the smaller geckos will avidly eat the fruit/nectar mixture mentioned in the day gecko account (page 164). We have also had girdle-tailed lizards eat the day gecko mixture. Certainly others will as well.

The veiled chameleon, *Chamaeleo calyptratus* ssp., a large representative of a group of lizards usually thought to be strictly insectivorous, eats a quite considerable percentage of leaves. In fact, the percentage of vegetation voluntarily taken by this lizard is so high that we have also mentioned them with the omnivorous lizards.

Although they are of immense interest to hobbyists, horned lizards have specialized diets and are difficult to successfully maintain in captivity. Pictured here is a Ditmar's horned lizard, Phrynosoma ditmarsii.

What we are saying, therefore, is that, despite the prevailing conventional wisdom, don't be afraid to experiment by adding some vegetation to the diets of even confirmed insectivores.

There are some insectivorous lizards that are so strongly myrmecophagus (ant-eating) that they make poor candidates for captive success. Among others are:

• Horned lizards *(Phrynosoma)*
• Thorny devils *(Moloch)*
• Flying dragons *(Draco)*
• Club-tailed tree iguanids *(Urocentron [Tropidurus])*
• Tree runners *(Plica [Tropidurus])*

We feel strongly that the members of these genera should not be either collected or purchased.

As with any other diet, it is best to provide a variety of insects for your lizards. Mealworms, waxworms, crickets, and other species are readily available commercially and discussed in the following pages.

The feed insects offered must be fresh and healthy, or your lizards will derive little benefit from them. Both "gut-load" and dust the insects you feed with D_3-calcium additives. These additives should be provided several times weekly for fast-growing baby lizards or for ovulating or egg-depositing females.

"Field plankton," wild insects gathered from insecticide-free pastures and fencerows with a sweep net and fed nearly immediately to your lizards, make an excellent and nutritious addition to a base diet of commercially available insects. Lizards quickly learn to pick their favorites from the melange, leaving behind the more unpalatable insect species.

The feed insects should be tailored to the size of the lizards being fed. Diminutive lizards such as reef and ashy geckos will thrive throughout their long lives on insects such as termites and pinhead (newly hatched) crickets. An adult broad-headed skink or eastern glass lizard will ignore such small fare, but will eagerly accept adults of crickets, giant mealworms, and sometimes earthworms.

Do not be surprised if your insectivorous lizard refuses to feed on mucous-laden fare, such as earthworms. Many insect eaters prefer the drier, more crunchy insects.

Some of the larger insectivorous lizards may augment their diet in the wild with an occasional nestling mouse. Captives may also eat an occasional mouse, with the emphasis being on "occasional."

For the moment, feeding of more than a very occasional nestling rodent seems contraindicated.

Raising Your Own Insects

You can control the quality of the food insects you offer your lizards. A poorly fed insect offers little but bulk as a food item. In contrast, a food insect that has fed on a variety of nutritious foods, particularly just before being offered as food to your insectivorous lizards, is a nutritional bonus package.

Foods to offer your feed insects include calcium, vitamin D_3, fresh fruit, grated carrots, squash, broccoli, fresh alfalfa and/or bean sprouts, honey, and vitamin/mineral-enhanced chick-laying mash. A commercially prepared gut-loading diet has only recently reached the pet marketplace.

Food insects that are commercially available include crickets, mealworms, giant mealworms, waxworms, fruitflies, butterworms, earthworms (not an insect, but a useful food item nonetheless). If you need large numbers, get dealer's names and phone numbers from hunting and fishing or reptile magazines or ask your reference librarian for this information and call your order in. If you need only small numbers of feed insects, your local pet or feed store will be your most economical route.

Breeding Insects

Here are some guidelines:

Crickets: The gray cricket (*Acheta domesticus*) is now bred commercially by the millions both

When captive, tiny insectivorous lizards such as this turnip-tailed gecko, Teratolepis fasciatus, *eat termites and pinhead crickets.*

for fishing bait and for pet food. Other species are readily collected in small numbers beneath debris in fields, meadows, and open woodlands. If available in suitable sizes, all species of crickets are ideal as a protein source for your lizard.

Feed your crickets the foods described above or a commercial gut-loading mix. Keep the food you offer fresh, even storing it in your refrigerator, and watch for any signs of mold. Crickets can and will be cannibalistic if crowded or underfed. While crickets will get much of the moisture requirements from their fruit and vegetables, they will also drink from a shallow water dish. To prevent their drowning, place cotton balls, a sponge, or even pebbles or aquarium gravel in a shallow water dish. These will give the crickets sufficient purchase to climb back out when they crawl in.

Favorites of many hobbyists, the various day geckos are ideal terrarium inhabitants. Here an ornate day gecko, Phelsuma ornata, laps honey-fruit mixture from a small dish.

If you choose to breed your own crickets, it is not difficult. Keep the cricket cage between 76 and 86°F (24–30°C). Place a shallow dish of slightly moistened sand, vermiculite or even cotton balls on the floor of the cage. The material in this dish will be the laying medium and will need to be kept very slightly moistened throughout the laying, incubation, and hatching process. Adult crickets are easily sexed. Females will have three "tubes" (the central one being the egg-depositing ovipositor) projecting from the rear of their bodies. Males lack the central ovipositor. The ovipositor is inserted into the laying medium and the eggs expelled. The eggs will hatch in 8 to 20 days, the duration being determined by cricket species and tank temperature. Nutritious food should always be available to the baby cricket.

Grasshoppers/locusts (*Locusta* sp. and *Shistocerca* sp. in part): Although migratory and other locusts are not commercially available in the United States, they are widely used as reptile foods in European and Asian countries. They can be bred or collected. Grasshoppers can be field collected in the United States by the deft wielding of a field net; however, grasshoppers are fast and may be difficult to collect.

In some southern areas, large, slow grasshoppers called "lubbers" can be found. Many of these have a brightly colored (often black and yellow or red) nymphal stage that

Keep crumpled newspapers, the center tubes from rolls of paper towels, or other such hiding areas in the cricket's cage. The paper towel tubes are useful, for they can be lifted out and the requisite number of crickets shaken from inside them into the cage or a transportation jar. This makes handling the fast-moving, agile insects easy. A tightly covered 20-gallon-long (75.7 L) tank will temporarily house 1,000 crickets. A substrate of sawdust, soil, vermiculite, or other such medium should be present. This must be changed often to prevent excessive odor from the insects.

can be fatally toxic to your lizards. The tan and buff adults seem to be less toxic but their use as a food item is contraindicated.

Offer your grasshoppers the insect diet and feed them to your lizards as quickly after they are collected as possible.

Waxworms (*Galleria* sp.): The "waxworm" is actually a caterpillar, the larval stage of the wax moth that frequently infests neglected beehives. Waxworms are available commercially from many sources. Check the ads in any reptile and amphibian magazine for wholesale distributors. Some pet shops or baitshops also carry waxworms.

Feed your waxworms chick-laying mash, wheat germ, honey, and yeast mixed into a syrupy paste.

Giant mealworms (*Zoophobas* sp.): These are the larvae of a South American beetle. They are rather new in the herpetocultural trade but are readily available from many sources. Check the ads in reptile magazines for the supplier closest to you. *Zoophobas* have proven to be of great value to reptile breeders.

Place your *Zoophobas* in shallow plastic trays containing an inch (25 mm) or so of sawdust. To breed them, place one mealworm each in a series of empty film canisters or other similar small containers that contain some sawdust and bran or oats. After a few days the worm will pupate, eventually metamorphosing into a fair-sized black beetle. The beetles can be placed together in a plastic tub or bin, containing a sawdust substrate and some old cracked limbs and twigs for egg laying. The female beetles deposit their eggs in the cracks in the limbs. The beetles and their larvae can be fed vegetables, fruits, oat, and bran. The mealworms will obtain all of their moisture requirements from the fresh vegetables and fruit.

Keep two colonies to assure that you have all sizes of the larvae you will need to offer your lizards. Although giant mealworms seem more easily digested by the lizards than common mealworms, neither species should be fed in excess. Most insectivorous lizards relish *Zoophobas* larvae. Fewer will eat the beetles.

Mealworms *(Tenebrio molitor):* Long a favorite of neophyte reptile and amphibian keepers, mealworms should actually be fed sparingly to your lizards. Mealworms are easily kept and bred in plastic or cardboard shoeboxes containing bran,

Although rather new on the market, silkworms are an excellent food source for many insectivorous lizards. The caterpillars are easily reared on prepared mulberry extract.

vegetables, and fruit for food and a potato or apple for their moisture requirements. It takes no special measures to breed these insects.

Roaches: Roaches, of one or more species, are present in much of the world. Several of the larger kinds are available in the pet market as insect pets. As a group, roaches are a natural food item that are relished by many lizards. Keep the roaches in a cage with a tight-fitting screened top, feed them the food mixture described above, and provide hiding places with paper towel tubes and crumpled pieces of newspaper. Clean the cage frequently. Raising your own roaches avoids the problem of offering roaches that have been exposed to insecticides.

Termites: Collect fresh as necessary. Should you decide to hold extras over, they may be kept in some of the slightly dampened wood in which you originally found them. Termites are most easily collected during the damp weather of spring and summer. It is definitely best to collect these insects as needed, then use them immediately. They are an excellent food insect for baby chameleons, small geckos, and other similarly sized lizards.

Diets for Carnivorous Lizards

Frequently seen examples of carnivorous lizards are:
• Most monitors
• Most tegus

Some of the lizards one might consider to be carnivorous—water dragons, sail-tailed dragons, and basilisks—are actually insectivorous or omnivorous. The truly carnivorous lizards tend to be active hunters, some of which are large enough to make any warm-blooded potential prey item nervous.

Certainly at some stage of their life, even predominantly carnivorous monitors and tegus seek other types of prey. Gray's monitor, Varanus *olivaceus,* of the Philippines also eats palm fruit and figs. Tegus of all sizes not only accept insects, but eat eggs and fruits as well.

Know the needs of your lizard! Unlike most monitors that are carnivorous, tiny Storr's monitors, Varanus storri *(top), feed primarily on insects while the large forest skink,* Lygosoma muelleri *(bottom), is an earthworm specialist.*

As captives, most of the larger monitors will do quite well on diets primarily of mice, rats, chicks, and quail. We feel that, as with all of the other feeding groups, variety is much better than exclusivity; thus, we feel that large monitors should also be offered fish, canned monitor and tegu foods, low-fat canned dog food, and other such fare. Like snakes, monitors that eat a whole-animal diet seem to need comparatively few vitamin and mineral supplements. This is particularly true if they are allowed to bask in natural, unfiltered sunlight. Fast-growing babies and ovulating or gravid females will need more calcium than adults.

Hobbyists have a tendency to feed monitors and tegus more than they actually need. The result can be grossly obese lizards, and obesity is a condition that is no better for reptiles than for humans. Moderate the diet; given adequate and varied diets, carnivorous lizard species will live for many years.

Although mice, rats, hamsters, and gerbils can be purchased commercially, they can be easily raised as well. You will probably need to seek chicks and quail from mail-order hatcheries.

Feeding and Raising Mice

Small prey animals (whether alive or dead) are often more readily accepted by a carnivorous lizards than large ones. Two small prey items are more easily digested by the lizard than one large food animal.

Small meals are also swallowed by monitors, tegus, and other such lizards more easily and quickly than a larger prey item. While this may make no difference to a well-adjusted specimen that feeds readily, if a nervous specimen or a poor feeder becomes stressed while eating, the lizard is apt to lose the urge to feed and disgorge a partially swallowed prey item.

Prekilled food items are suggested. A live rodent may injure or startle even a large lizard, resulting in either stress or irreversible damage.

Frozen mice: You can generally buy bulk lots of frozen mice from a reptile or reptile food dealer and thaw the number needed in warm water (blot them dry with paper towels at feeding time) or thaw the mice beneath a basking lamp. Because of hot spots, partial cooking, and deterioration of the body wall, the use of a microwave for thawing mice is *not recommended*.

Force feeding: Despite all of your efforts, there is the occasional lizard that will not voluntarily accept any offered food item. In these cases there is little recourse but to

An omnivorous lizard, the little shield-tailed agama eats small insects and leafy greens.

force feed the specimen. Remember, the digestive system of a lizard that has not fed in some time is probably compromised. Do not overfeed such a specimen. In fact, initially *underfeed* it. A compromised, basically nonfunctioning digestive system will be better able to digest a proportionately small meal than a large one. In force feeding, you may use a "pinky pump," a metal syringe with a large diameter "needle" through which, when the plunger is depressed, the parts of prekilled pinky mice or vitamin-fortified meat baby food are forced into the lizard, or you may actually force (massage) a small food animal down the lizard's throat.

In either case, force feeding is traumatic for your pet and requires the utmost care on your part. Move *slowly!* This is important, for a startled lizard is quite apt to fight the force feeding or to regurgitate the meal once it *is* force fed.

Do remember that the lizard will have to be mostly immobilized.

Lubricate the tip of the pinky pump before inserting it down the throat (into the esophagus) of the specimen. The unenhanced length of the tip of the pinky pump will allow sufficient insertion to feed a small lizard. If the pump is being used to feed a larger specimen, it may be necessary to affix a longer piece of smooth plastic tube to allow insertion for an additional distance. Use care. Do not injure the gums, teeth, or mouth-lining of the lizard when forcibly opening its

mouth or during the process of force feeding.

If you decide to use a small prekilled mouse as the meal, first lubricate the mouse with water (some hobbyists prefer egg white). Next, after propping the lizard's mouth open with a padded tongue depressor (or other such instrument), insert the rodent, head first, gently into the mouth of the lizard. If done slowly and gently, the lizard will probably not fight this procedure too hard.

If at any time that you are doing this your lizard begins to voluntarily swallow, slowly release your grip and allow the animal to eat voluntarily. Often, however, the reluctant feeder will volunteer nothing and it will be necessary to slowly work the prey animal into and beyond its throat. Once pushed gently past the angle of the lizard's mouth, you will be able to work the rodent downward by gently massaging the throat anterior to the food item. If the lizard shows little resistance, gently remove the prop (this, in itself, can be quite a challenge) and release the lizard. Often, at that point, the lizard will continue swallowing. If it begins to try to regurgitate, gently grasp the animal and massage the prey a little further down.

Even force feeding may not always save a seriously debilitated lizard, but it *is* worth making the effort.

Using food rodents: Mice, rats, and other rodents, are rather generally available at pet shops and specialty dealers across the United States, Europe, and in many areas of Asia. Often, food rodents and lizards are considerably cheaper than pet rodents or lizards. Frozen rodents may be cheaper yet. Compare prices.

Because of the ease with which domestic mice and rats can be obtained, there is a tendency for hobbyists to try to use them as an exclusive food. While this may be acceptable to some species, it is probably not natural, and dietary variety is better.

We are often asked about the wisdom of feeding wild rodents (especially mice) to monitors and tegus. We feel that there are three points that you should consider when making a decision:

1. You must be absolutely certain that the wild rodent has ingested no rat or mouse poisons.
2. Be aware that wild rodents can be carriers of certain serious diseases that are transmissible to humans.
3. Once they have eaten wild rodents, some lizards like them so much that they may be reluctant to accept domestic types again.

On the positive side, some lizards that are reluctant to eat, or even non-feeders on domestic rodents may eagerly accept wild rodent species.

Breeding Your Own Food Rodents

Although readily available at pet and specialty shops, or in large quantities from mail-order dealers, some persons choose to breed their own food rodents. Most are easily bred, but do breed best if maintained at comfortable room temperatures. If too cold or too hot, breeding ceases or, if it continues, litters are smaller and cannibalism of the newborns is likely. Of all rodents, mice are the most easily bred and the most universally accepted by carnivorous lizards. A single male to three or four female mice can be housed in a 10-gallon (37.85 L) tank or a rodent breeding cage. A colony such as this will produce a rather steady supply of babies that can be fed to your smaller specimens, or allowed to size for the larger specimens. The mouse colony will produce a distinct odor. If indoors, it will probably be necessary to clean the cages at least twice weekly. Since even clean cages often have a distinct odor, it is better to breed mice away from your home if possible. A temperature-controlled garage is often ideal for a colony or two. Use aspen or pine shavings for the bedding. *Do not* use cedar bedding for your mice; the phenols contained in cedar can be harmful to your lizards. Feed your mice either a "lab-chow" diet that is specifically formulated for them or a healthy mixture of seeds and vegetables. Fresh water must be available at all times. Lizards will derive the most benefit from healthy prey.

Gerbils and hamsters can also be raised in small cages. Rats will do better in somewhat larger facilities.

Certain wild mice can also be bred in captivity. Among the most frequently seen of these are deer and white-footed mice.

Diets for Omnivorous Lizards

Frequently seen examples of omnivorous lizards are:
• Bearded dragons
• Blue-tongued skinks
• Cunningham's skinks
• Day geckos
• Knight anoles
• New Caledonian geckos
• Racerunners
• Tegus
• Veiled chameleons
• Water dragons
• Whiptails

There are more lizards that are omnivorous—consuming both animal and plant materials—than strict herbivores.

Among the omnivores are species such as the larger species of bearded dragons, many skinks (including the egernine skinks—Cunningham's, blue-tongued, etc.), tegus, racerunners and whiptails, some anoles, water dragons, and so on. Species from groups that we have long thought of as being entirely carnivorous occasionally surprise us. Among these are the Philippine Gray's monitor that eats a preponderance of figs and other fruits, and the Yemen veiled chameleon that eagerly seeks out and eats leaves and blossoms.

Pollens, nectar, and sap are necessary components in the diets of the day, New Caledonian, and some other geckos. They will need these, or a suitable substitute in captivity. For suggestions on formulating a diet for the day geckos see page 164.

Assuredly there are other lizards that, if given the chance, will surprise us. We urge you to not only peruse the species accounts in this book, but to check the diets suggested in species-specific books as well. We further suggest that you experiment on your own by keeping a portion of day gecko fruit diet, leaves, and blossoms available to your various lizards. You may well find that they enjoy the variety you provide.

Food in the Wild Versus Food in Captivity

In the wild, omnivorous lizards accept molluscs, carrion, insects, anellids, crustaceans, berries and other available fruits, and some greenery, plant saps, and pollens. In captivity, most—large and small alike—will eat good-quality canned cat and/or reptile foods as well as bananas, strawberries, blueberries, kiwi fruit, melon, insects, and suitably sized rodents. Romaine, kale, bok choy, turnip and collard greens, even the leaves of some house plants will also be accepted.

Dietary variety, *not* simply convenience for us, seems the keynote to long-term success in lizard keeping. For example, although they are readily available (and readily eaten), a diet exclusively of mice is not suitable for blue-tongued skinks. Nor, although they will accept insects, is a diet exclusively of crickets suitable for a day gecko.

Providing a lizard with the care it truly needs, whether a $2.00 anole or a $1,000 frilled lizard, is a commitment that we must take very seriously. We must learn as much as we can about the species we choose, then strive to learn more through practical (and anecdotal) experience. Nor should we depend entirely on the lizard to do what is best. The essentially herbivorous green iguana is a perfect example. Captive iguanas will readily, even preferentially, eat insects, mice, and prepared animal protein—and those that do almost invariably break down with gout or kidney problems later in life. Captive iguanas that are denied animal protein seem more apt to live long, disease-free lives.

The same may well be true for lizards that are normally omnivorous, but surely the latitude for error will be greater. It is unlikely that a blue-tongued skink (a species that may normally eat 50 percent or more animal protein) that is denied vegetation in its diet will be adversely affected as quickly as an iguana would. The same is true of inland bearded dragons for which a normal diet apparently consists of about 75 percent animal protein. But we should insist that our charges eat a diet that is healthy for them, while skewing dietary offer-

Some lizards, such as this baby fire skink, Mochlus fernandii, *will accept prepared foods in addition to insects, fruit, and vegetables.*

ings in the direction that would be normal for them.

There is speculation that if pinky mice rather than insects are provided to a normally insectivorous lizard, adverse lipid (fat) buildups can occur. This again points to the need for normalcy and variety in a lizard's diet.

Despite the claims to the contrary, some veterinarians feel that the canned "complete diets" currently on the market, may not be the best for your lizards. Again, we urge variety.

Chapter Five
Handling Your Lizards

To Handle or Not to Handle—That Is the Question

When most people acquire a lizard of any kind, they do so with the thought of the creature becoming a "pet."

A pet is literally, "a domesticated animal kept for pleasure rather than utility." So, at the outset, we see that a lizard does not actually qualify as a pet, for there simply are no lizard species that are truly domesticated. A very few are bred in some numbers in captivity; fewer yet are "farmed" in fairly large numbers for the pet or hide trade, or as food, but none are domesticated. In fact, even today, most lizards that enter the pet trade are collected directly from the wild. They are caught in pitfall traps, netted, noosed, by hand, or by other methods, but most are from the wild.

Escape Ploys

In the wild, a caught lizard is usually a dead lizard, a food item for a larger predator, so over the eons lizards have become adept at avoiding capture and almost equally adept at escaping if they are unfortunate enough to be caught. In these escape efforts, lizards bite, autotomize their tail, slap with their tail, smear their cloacal contents, wriggle strongly, become catatonic, change color, inflate their body or throat, or even tear big patches of their body skin free. These escape ploys may be used singly or in combination, and some can be pretty effective.

So, actually, those lizards that we have as pets are those that have failed dismally in their flight for freedom—but at least they're not dead—not yet, anyway. And although none of us can tell for certain what any lizard is thinking, we don't have to be particularly astute to know, by merely a glimpse at their body language, that most lizards simply do not like to be handled. At the approach of a hand (in their eyes a gigantic predator), they become defensive, attempt to escape, or, if cornered and frightened, close their eyes and assume an attitude of rigidity. Seldom will a lizard merely go about its business and allow itself to be handled.

Lizards Are Loners

By nature, the males of most lizards are solitary and territorial

Some lizards, like this young green iguana, adapt well to handling and are so lackadaisical that they will even eat while being held.

creatures. This does not mean that several (of some species) will not coexist in a few square yards of ideal habitat, but usually individual territories are well defined and vigorously defended within this range. Males of other lizard species may be distressed if they are even within view of another example of their own species and sex. Males are more aggressive during the breeding season than at other times. Females of most species, while not actually gregarious, are usually not as persistently territorial and asocial as the males.

The very fact that lizards are loners precludes them becoming truly good pets in the usual sense of the word. Allowing themselves to be grasped is entirely alien to them.

But some lizard species are a little less frenetic than others in their efforts to escape and some individual lizards are quieter than others. Generally speaking, larger specimens are often less stressed by handling than smaller examples, but even then there is both species and individual variation. And, if a larger lizard does decide to scratch or bite the handler, the result of a cursory effort can be more severe than that of a small lizard. Bites and scratches by the bacteria-laden jaws and claws of carnivorous lizards (especially those not kept quite as clean as they should be) are more apt to cause infection than those of herbivorous species. Remember, these lizards gobble down carrion and they never brush

Day geckos should not be handled. Even when gently and carefully held the skin may tear badly.

their teeth. *If your skin is broken, cleaning, disinfecting, and treating the abrasion or wound is very important.* The wound site should be carefully monitored and, no matter how severe, medical assistance sought if swelling, lividity, or increasing pain follow.

Why Keep Lizards?

By now you are probably asking: "Why would I (or anyone else) keep a lizard?" To this our answer would be: "Because they're beautiful, interesting and, if you can accept them on their own terms (in most cases a 'just look, don't touch' kind of pet), they can provide you with years of companionship."

This is our outlook. We keep lizards as terrarium animals, taking pride and delight in providing them with the husbandry parameters necessary to induce long-term

health, "happiness," and breeding behavior. The keeping of reptiles and amphibians is, for us, a learning experience. We respect what *we* think to be the preferences of our charges, and have no real urge to handle even those specimens that might allow us to do so.

Handling Methods

Yes, there are some lizards that are often, or at least occasionally, handleable. This is especially so if you don't just suddenly reach toward them and try to grab them. Always move slowly but decisively. Leopard and fat-tailed geckos can be shepherded into the palm of your hand where they will usually sit quietly (be sure you don't drop them; they can be easily injured!). Blue-tongued, pink-tongued, shingle-backed, and some other skinks can actually be slowly grasped and gently lifted. Support them with your other hand. *Some* (but most definitely not all) green iguanas and many water dragons will allow you to lift them if they are approached slowly from a place at or beneath their perching level. In many cases, once they become accustomed to you, these lizards will climb rather confidently onto an extended hand or arm, or even ride on your shoulder. Don't take them outside when they are not restrained. If frightened they will drop to the ground and scuttle quickly away. Unlike the terrestrial leopard geckos, the arboreal green iguanas and water dragons can drop considerable distances without injuring themselves. This escape technique is often used by both young and adult aboreal lizards. They drop from a tree limb or rock face into the water or surrounding foliage and swim or run away to escape a predator.

Attitudes of lizards toward being handled can suddenly change. An iguana (especially a male), for example, may be perfectly tractable when young, but entirely unmanageable during periods of hormonal stimulation when sexually mature. At this time of each year, it is more than ever a clear case of dominate or be dominated. Dominant males get to breed the females; subordinate males often do not. To be a dominant male, one must be the undisputed "king of the mountain." If disputed, whether by another lizard or by an owner's approaching hand, the dominant lizard must vanquish. This is a stressful time for your lizard, and since prolonged stress is decidedly unhealthy for the lizard, suitable compromises must be reached.

Access to unfiltered, natural sunlight can also stimulate normal, natural "don't you dare touch me" behavior. This is well documented in the venomous Gila monster, a lizard that is often (in fact, usually) docile and benign when deprived of ultraviolet rays, but that can become an enthusiastic antagonist when ultraviolet is provided. Similar behavioral changes have been noted in iguanas, monitors, skinks, and other lizard species.

Thus, the message here is that not all lizards are handleable and even those that usually are may not be so under all circumstances. Through its body language your lizard will advise you of its "moods," and "mood swings." If you learn them and heed them, you both will be happier for it.

Chapter Six
Lizard Health

Respiratory Disorders

Although well-acclimated, properly maintained lizards are not prone to respiratory ailments, stressed new imports and marginally healthy specimens, and those subjected to unnatural periods of cold (especially damp-cold), may occasionally develop "colds" or pneumonia. Some respiratory disorders may also be associated with the weakening brought about by a heavy endoparasite burden.

Respiratory ailments are indicated by sneezing, lethargic demeanor, and unnaturally rapid, often shallow, breathing. As the disease progresses, rasping and bubbling may accompany each of your lizard's breaths. At this stage the respiratory condition is often critical and can be fatal.

Begin by elevating the temperature of the basking area (*not* the entire cage) to about 100°F (37.8°C). Lizards, as a group, are dependent upon outside heat sources for their metabolic rate. The more optimum (variable by species) the surroundings, the better able the specimen is to deal with a respiratory problem.

The rest of the cage should be retained at that considered optimal for the species in question when healthy. If the symptoms of respiratory distress do not greatly lessen within a day or two, do not delay. Take your lizard to the veterinarian for diagnosis and appropriate treatment. Respiratory conditions may be due to bacterial or viral infections, or to lungworms or other parasites, allergies, or tumors. Correct diagnosis is important.

There are many "safe" drugs available, but some respiratory problems do not respond well to these. The newer aminoglycoside drugs and others, newer still, are more effective, but correspondingly more dangerous. There is little latitude in dosage amounts and the lizard *must* be well hydrated to ensure against renal (kidney) damage. Some reptile veterinarians feel the injection site for aminoglycosides should be *anterior* to mid-body to avoid damaging the kidneys.

Endoparasites

The presence of internal parasites in lizards from the wild is a foregone conclusion. Your lizard

Medical Treatments for Internal Parasites

Because of the complexities of identification of endoparasites and the necessity to accurately weigh specimens to be treated, the eradication of internal parasites is best left to a qualified reptile veterinarian. Here are a few of the recommended medications and dosages:

Amoebas and **Trichomonads:** 40–50 mg/kg of **Metronidazole** orally. The treatment is repeated in two weeks.

Dimetridazole can also be used but the dosage is very different: 40–50 mg/kg of Dimetrizadole is administered daily for five days; the treatment is then repeated in two weeks. All treatments with both medications are administered once daily.

Coccidia: Many treatments are available.

The dosages of **sulfadiazine, sulfamerazine,** and **sulfamethazine** are identical. Administer 75 mg/kg the first day, then follow up for the next five days with 45 mg/kg.

All treatments orally and once daily.

Sulfadimethoxine is also effective. The initial dosage is 90 mg/kg orally to be followed on the next five days with 45 mg/kg orally. All dosages are administered once daily.

Trimethoprim-sulfa may also be used. 30 mg/kg should be administered once daily for 7 days.

Cestodes (Tapeworms): Several effective treatments are available.

Bunamidine may be administered orally at a dosage of 50 mg/kg. A second treatment occurs in 14 days.

Niclosamide, orally, at a dosage of 150 mg/kg, is also effective. A second treatment is given in two weeks.

Praziquantel may be administered either orally or intramuscularly. The dosage is 5–8 mg/kg and is to be repeated in 14 days.

Trematodes (Flukes):

Praziquantel at 8 mg/kg may be administered either orally or intramuscularly. The treatment is repeated in 2 weeks.

Nematodes (Roundworms): Several effective treatments are available.

Levamisole, an injectible intraperitoneal treatment, should be administered at a dosage of 10 mg/kg and the treatment repeated in 2 weeks.

Ivermectin, injected intramuscularly in a dosage of 200 mcg/kg is effective. The treatment is to be repeated in two weeks. Ivermectin can be toxic to certain taxa.

Thiabendazole and **Fenbendazole** have similar dosages. Both are administered orally at 50-100 mg/kg and repeated in 14 days.

Mebendazole is administered orally at a dosage of 20–25 mg/kg and repeated in 14 days.

may be host to roundworms, pinworms and other nematodes, tapeworms, and/or parasitic protozoans. We feel that whether or not the lizard is treated for endoparasites depends on the behavior of each individual lizard. Certainly the problems created by endoparasitic loads in weakened lizards need to be addressed promptly.

If the specimen in question is bright-eyed, alert, feeding well, and has a good color, you may wish to forego an immediate veterinary assessment. Endoparasitic loads can actually diminish if you keep the cage of your specimen scrupulously clean, thereby preventing reinfestation.

Getting rid of endoparasites requires administering a substance that is toxic to the parasites in dosages that will not harm your lizard. Obviously, since dosages must be accurate, you need to take your animal to your veterinarian. It is very easy for a layperson to miscalculate metric conversions or to fail to actually get the correct dosage into the lizard. The result can be fatal or futile. Let your reptile veterinarian do the work for which he or she was trained.

Nowhere is the need for selecting a veterinarian well versed in reptile biology and treatment more valid than when determining whether or not to purge a lizard of its endoparasites.

In most cases, with most animals, if endoparasites are present, a veterinarian will be quick to recommend their elimination. Such purging may well be best for the majority of reptiles and amphibians. However, with herbivorous reptiles such as chuckwallas, iguanas, and spiny-tailed agamids *(Uromastyx),* etc., at least some of the various microbes and nematodes present in the gut are instrumental in the cellulose breakdown of ingested plant material, but an inordinate proliferation of these same creatures can be quickly fatal.

Ectoparasites

External parasites are less problematic to treat than endoparasites. Mites and ticks are certainly easier to "diagnose" than internal parasites and, of the two, we have found mites to be far less common.

Mites are less-than-pinhead-size dots, frequently found near the lizard's eyes. Ticks are larger parasites, about an eighth- to one-quarter inch (3.2–6.4 mm) across. When empty they are deflated and seedlike, and rounded and bladderlike when engorged.

Treatment

Use a commercial reptile mite insecticide for mites on lizards, and follow the instructions exactly.

There are now several sprays available that have an Ivermectin base. Again we stress that treatment instructions *must* be followed exactly. We also suggest that permanent water dishes be removed during treatment. Provide water daily for your lizards but remove it again after the lizards drink. This will prevent contamination of the water by the insecticide. Consult a reptile-oriented veterinarian when possible.

It is best if ticks are removed singly whenever they are seen. They imbed their mouthparts deeply when feeding, and if merely pulled from the lizard these may break off in the wound. It is best to first dust them individually with Sevin powder, then return a few minutes later and pull the ticks off gently with a pair of tweezers.

Other Maladies

Several other diseases and maladies may rarely occur. Among these are:

Mineralization of Internal Organs

This is caused by over-supplementing with calcium. Known as *hypercalycemia,* a treatment has now been developed but it is both lengthy and expensive; it requires about two weeks of treating and monitoring by a veterinarian. There is a fine line between too much and not enough calcium and vitamin D_3. Once diagnosed and corrected you'll need to reduce both calcium and D_3 intake by your lizard. If untreated or too far advanced, this can be fatal.

Hypoglycemia

Hypoglycemia relates to low blood sugar; stress or pancreatic dysfunction can be the causative agent. The stress factor is correctable; the pancreatic dysfunction, most commonly caused by an insulin secreting tumor, usually is not. Hyperglycemia, or diabetes mellitus, is more commonly seen and is treated with insulin.

Chapter Seven

Conditioning and Breeding Your Lizards

Although many lizards in very diverse groups breed well in captivity with little concerted preparation, other species may prove very difficult and require exacting cycling. The term *cycling,* as we use it, refers to a physiological readying of your lizard for breeding.

Species such as basilisks, bearded dragons, blue-tongued skinks, leopard geckos, and many of the day geckos are easily bred. Other species such as collared lizards, bent-toed geckos, and plated lizards/zonosaurs are more difficult. Record and share your methods, successes, and even failures.

Cycling

Under natural conditions, the life cycles of lizards are influenced by seasonal climatic changes. Influencing factors include photoperiod, temperature, rainfall, and relative humidity. These annual seasonal changes can (and if you hope to breed some of the more demanding

lizard species, *must*) be duplicated in the terrarium.

Photoperiod

Photoperiod can be easily duplicated by using a timer to turn terrarium lights on and off at dawn and dusk. This can also be done manually. Check the weather page in your local newspaper for the exact sunrise and sunset times, and make notes of these changes for future breeding seasons. Be patient—it may take specimens imported from southern latitudes a season or two to acclimate to the reversed seasons of northern latitude herpetoculturists, and vice versa.

Temperatures and Humidity

Temperatures, both daily and seasonal, can be altered with the prudent use of lights and/or heating elements. Temperatures for tropical lizard species should be allowed to drop slightly on summer nights and slightly more during the shortest days of the year. Some tropical lizards may actually require a month or so of semihibernation during the winter months to attain reproductive readiness. Temperate lizards may require up to four months of full hibernation.

Rainfall can be simulated and seasonally altered by expedient misting techniques. Generally speaking, an afternoon misting during the spring breeding season serves as a trigger for breeding behavior.

Relative humidity within the cage can be altered by partially or completely covering the terrarium top with glass, plexiglass, or sheet plastic, or by covering or removing plastic covering from outdoor or wire and wood frame cages.

For the most part you should strive to have the lowest humidity, the fewest hours of daylight, and the lowest temperatures in midwinter (this holds true for both temperate and tropical lizard species). The greatest amount of all three would be provided in midsummer.

Your lizards should be fed most heavily during the long, warm, humid days of summer. As you allow the temperatures to cool, reduce the feeding, both in quantity at a given meal and in frequency. When temperatures again warm, increase meal size and frequency. Be sure to provide plenty of calcium and D_3 throughout the year. These additives are especially important at the time of eggshell formation by adult female geckos and for proper bone development and the growth of hatchlings and juveniles.

Parthenogenesis

Although most lizards reproduce bisexually, some whiptails, lacertas, geckos, and others reproduce parthenogenetically. *Parthenogenesis* involves the production of viable eggs by a female without benefit of male fertilization; the young produced are almost always females. Ovulation is stimulated by female/female pseudocourtship and coupling.

There don't seem to be any real advantages to parthenogenesis, other than the fact that any two properly cycled and stimulated lizards can each produce young. Actually, current scholarly trends are that vertebrate parthenogenesis is not as effective a means of reproduction in the long run as heterosexuality, simply because there is no genetic mixing.

The Eggs

The vast majority of lizards are *oviparous;* that is, they reproduce by laying eggs. However, depending on the species, the eggs may have hard, calcareous shells or pliable (and permeable) parchment-like shells. Again depending on the species, a clutch may consist of a single egg (reef geckos) to several dozen eggs (tegus).

Lizards that produce their young alive are termed *ovoviviparous* (have no placental nourishment) or *viviparous* (have placental nourishment). These species may also

Tens of thousands of leopard geckos are bred annually in both commercial and hobbyists' facilities. These eggs are being incubated and hatched at The Gourmet Rodent. A hatchling leopard gecko has pipped the egg and is emerging. Hatchlings are strongly banded and begin foraging for tiny insects when only several days old. Make sure the incubator has an adjustable thermostat.

have clutches of one baby (giant prehensile-tailed skink) to more than two dozen babies (eastern blue-tongued skink).

Choosing the Deposition Site

In nature, female lizards may choose arboreal (broad-headed skinks), rock-face (many geckos), or terrestrial (basilisks) deposition sites.

In some cases, especially where suitable deposition sites are difficult to find, females may nest communally. Some lizards may merely scatter their eggs in leaf litter, preparing no actual nest. The eggs may be hard-shelled adhesive, hard-shelled nonadhesive, and soft-shelled nonadhesive. Like the egg layers, females of live-bearing lizards may give birth in terrestrial situations (shingle-backed skinks), amidst rock exfoliations (girdle-tailed lizards), or in trees (chameleons).

Arboreal sites can be used by both egg-gluing and non-egg-gluing lizard species. Captive egg gluers may place their eggs on terrarium glass or the leaves of stiff-leafed plants; non-gluers will often use the central rosettes of plants such as sanseverias or bromeliads for deposition sites.

Egg Incubation—
An Overview

Following deposition, remove the eggs as soon as possible for incubation. It seems best, but may not be as critical as we once thought, if the orientation in which the egg was found is not changed. (In other words, just to be safe, keep the same side up.)

Egg gluers: If the eggs are produced by an egg-gluing species, the eggs may be placed in irremovable situations (such as on terrarium glass). You'll need to tape a small plastic cup containing a little moistened sphagnum over the eggs, taking care that the moss does not actually come in contact with the eggs. Remoisten the moss as needed.

Vermiculite: If you use vermiculite as a medium for incubation, moisten it with four parts of water to six parts of vermiculite (by weight). Place an inch (25 mm) or so in the bottom of a deli or similar plastic cup. The eggs may be placed directly on, or half

Captive females of most chameleon species need several inches of dirt in which they can dig their nest. This is a veiled chameleon. After incubating for about 6 months, a hatchling veiled chameleon emerges from the egg.

buried in, this substrate. Place the lid loosely on the cup and put the cup in the incubator. A shallow open dish of water in the incubator will help keep the relative humidity at 100 percent.

Sphagnum: If sphagnum is used, it should be thoroughly moistened, then squeezed as dry as possible

In nature, hatchlings of the tokay gecko, Gekko gecko, emerge from adhesive eggs placed high on the side of a building or in the hollow of a tree.

cess also seems greater with these eggs when they are kept from directly touching the dampened substrate.

Sex determination: The sex of many lizard species is determined by the temperature at which the egg is incubated. This is called "temperature-dependent sex determination." Cool temperatures produce females; overly warm ones will produce males. For most lizards, incubation temperatures of 83 to 87°F (28–30.6°C) will produce hatchlings of both sexes.

by hand. The eggs can be nestled directly amidst the moss.

Soft-shelled eggs: The eggs of the eublepharine and diplodactyline geckos as well as those of most other lizards are soft-shelled and permeable. These eggs are capable of both desiccation or overhydration. Keep an eye on these eggs while they incubate. If they get slick, decrease the moisture inside the incubator. If the medium gets a little dry, add water to it.

Hard-shelled eggs: Some rain forest and other humidland gecko species produce hard-shelled eggs. These will hatch best if kept from directly touching the substrate. Place them on a small plastic lid or other such support. They will require a 90 to 100 percent relative humidity to develop properly. The hard-shelled eggs of many aridland gecko species will best develop at a 45 to 60 percent relative humidity. Hatching suc-

Making Your Own Incubator

Materials needed for one incubator:
- one wafer thermostat/heater (obtainable from feed stores; these are commonly used in incubators for chicks)
- one thermometer
- one styrofoam cooler with thick sides (a fish shipping box is ideal)
- one "heat tape" (the type used to prevent outdoor pipes from freezing)

1. Poke a hole through the lid of the styrofoam cooler, and affix/suspend the thermostat/heater from the inside. Connect the heat tape to the thermostat terminals. Add another hole for a thermometer, so you can check on the inside temperature without opening the top. If there's no flange on the thermometer to

keep it from slipping through the hole in the lid, use a rubber band wound several times around the thermometer to form a flange.

2. Put the lid on the cooler, and plug in the thermostat/heater. Wait half an hour and check the temperature. Adjust the thermostat/heater until the temperature inside the incubator is about 80 to 86°F (26.7–30°C) (see the species accounts, beginning on page 64, so you'll know what temperature to use). The L-pin "handle" on the top of the thermostat controls the rheostat setting. Once you have the temperature regulated, put the container of eggs inside the incubator and close the lid.

3. Check the temperature daily and add a little water to the incubating medium as needed. The preferred humidity varies by species between 65 and 100 percent. This

Unlike the brilliantly striped hatchlings, the adults of the broad-headed skink, Plestiodon laticeps, *are an overall warm brown and breeding males have an orange head.*

can be accomplished by keeping the hatching medium damp to the touch but too dry to yield water when squeezed by your hand.

Chapter Eight

Big Lizards, Big Cages

Green Iguanas

Description: Throughout this book you will find references to the green iguana, *Iguana iguana*. At one time, this was an immensely popular lizard with about 2,000,000 babies being sold annually in the United States. They are available at nearly every pet shop in the country, but perhaps they should *not* be, for green iguanas can be quite a problem to keep and to keep well.

Buy iguanas that have been captive bred and hatched whenever they are available. Although it is true that many imports are now "farmed," most domestically raised iguanas are less stressed than imports and, although they may be a little more expensive than imports, will host fewer parasites (or may, perhaps, be—temporarily—parasite free).

Keeping: A proper diet for these lizards is extremely important. Although many iguanas will consume insects and even an occasional baby mouse, long-term studies have proven that the healthiest and longest living iguanas are those that are fed a nutritional and varied vegetable diet (see pages 34–39), which can be augmented with a little fruit. Always think "veggie" for your iguana; this will save your lizard from a bout with gout or kidney dysfunction.

Know that vitamin D_3 and calcium are mandatory additives for iguanas of all ages. This is especially true during periods of rapid growth and if your specimen does not have access to unfiltered, natural sunlight. Ultraviolet rays (UV-B) are necessary to promote the synthesizing of vitamin D_3 and metabolism of calcium by your iguana. Less D_3 and calcium is necessary when access to unfiltered, natural sunlight is allowed. An ample calcium level is *mandatory* for bone development and prevention of metabolic bone disease. Note that high levels of phosphorus will offset the benefits of calcium. Approximately twice as much calcium as phosphorus should be present in any additives and three to four times more calcium than phosphorus is better yet.

Remember also that if it is a male, and properly cared for, that ten-inch-long (25 cm) baby iguana that you are choosing today can be a four-foot-long (1.22 m) lizard in 24 months. When hormones start

churning at sexual maturity, that same tame iguana can become very bad tempered. To determine if you have a male or female green iguana, check the femoral pores along the underside of the hind legs—males have larger, more easily discernable pores. They have more massive heads, larger crests, and are slightly heavier in build than females—all qualities hard to differentiate in hatchling-sized babies.

To even begin to do it justice, an adult iguana needs a cage at least 8 feet × 8 feet × 6 feet (2.44 m × 2.44 m × 1.83 m), or even a room dedicated to its housing. An iguana needs access to ultraviolet light, basking hot spots, a year round warm temperature and, somewhere along the line, no matter how good the regimen of care you give it, your iguana will probably need to see a

veterinarian. Not all veterinarians are comfortable with or qualified to treat reptilian disorders. Dosages and administration of medications, even the medications themselves, can be very different from those used for birds and mammals. Do not wait until your iguana is sick to find a suitable, *reptile-qualified,* veterinarian.

Breeding: Iguanas can be bred in captivity. Besides having both sexes present, it will be necessary that the lizards be kept in large enough facilities and be "cycled" properly (see pages 58–59).

While neotropical green iguanas do not undergo extended periods of dormancy, they do experience certain annual climatic changes. For the more northerly ranging iguanas these changes include, among others, slightly reduced hours of winter daylight, slightly lowered winter nighttime temperatures, reduced winter relative humidity and a lessening of rain activity during the winter months. The climatic changes are even less pronounced in the more tropical areas, being largely limited to a reduction of humidity and shower activity during the winter months. Slight though these changes may be, they stimulate the hormonal changes which trigger breeding.

As breeding readiness is neared, an increased production of testosterone will stimulate more pronounced territoriality displays and an increasingly aggressive attitude toward both rival males and the people who care for the lizards.

"Tame," content and healthy iguanas that are familiar with their cages make the best breeders. The courtship ritual of a male green iguana is characterized by pushups, head bobs and nods and repeated dewlap distensions. Following this ritual, the male will mount the female, retaining position by grasping her nape with his jaws. The male will curve and angle his body around that of the female until cloacae are juxtapositioned. When their bodies are correctly positioned, intromission is usually quickly accomplished and is accompanied by a varied series of movements, including a "shrugging" sequence. After breeding is completed, the iguanas again go their separate ways. Successful breedings will result in the female depositing a clutch of from 25 to 65 eggs about 45 days later. An incubation temperature between 83 and 88°F is suitable; 86°F (±1 degree) seems best.

After choosing a suitable site, the female iguana will dig a deep nest. The dirt and debris loosened with the forefeet is removed with the rear feet. During nest preparation in the wild, a female iguana is particularly vulnerable to predators. If the female is disturbed during the nest digging, or if the female encounters roots or rocks, the female will often leave to begin anew elsewhere. Even if completed, the female iguana may ultimately decide that the nesting chamber is unsuitable and may proceed anew at another location and another time.

However, if the completed nest is satisfactory, after resting, the female will lay her clutch and fill the hole with the dirt she has removed. When incubating conditions are ideal, the eggs may hatch in about 70 days. Under cooler, dryer conditions the incubation duration may near a full three months.

In Dade County, Florida, feral iguanas have been seen breeding, (temperatures allowing), from early mid-February to late May. Nesting activities have been noted in the months of April, May, June, and July. Hatchlings have been found throughout the calendar months of summer. In that seasonally dry, almost xeric area, females tend to construct their nests beneath moisture retaining roadside trash such as cardboard, boards or discarded mattresses.

Iguanas kept out-of-doors in the southernmost areas of our country can be allowed to breed and nest nearly like they would in the wild. We, as owners, merely need to ascertain that suitable nesting areas are present in the cages. In some of the more ideally arranged cages, the female iguana will construct her own nest in much the way she would in the wild. If she does not initially begin her own nest (and you feel the substrate is suitable) merely disturbing the surface of the ground may be an adequate prompt. Where substrate conditions are unsuitable, either a nesting chamber must be constructed for the female iguana or an artificial nesting site provided.

Several nest models seem equally well-accepted by gravid female iguanas. Suitability seems governed by four considerations: adequate amounts of space, adequate amount of darkness, appropriate moisture content and appropriate temperature.

An "in ground" nest can be made by either digging down and framing an adequately-sized depression with wood or by sinking the inverted bottom third of a large, dark-colored (dark brown or black), heavy plastic trash can in the ground. In either case an entryway must be left open. It will be necessary to cover the wooden chamber with a piece of plywood or other suitably opaque top. Although many breeders feel that iguanas favor rather long, tunnel-like entryways to their in-ground nesting chambers, these are certainly not mandatory. However, should you decide to provide one, it is easily made by burying one or more lengths of ceramic pipe of suitable diameter (end to end if more than a single piece is used), sloping them from the surface to the entrance of the main nesting chamber.

An above ground nest can be easily made by utilizing a large, dark-colored, rigid plastic trash can. A can with four flat sides is the easiest to work with. Choose an area of the pen where the can will not overheat. Lay the can on its side and cut an entryhole in an upper corner of the lid. Securely affix the lid to the bottom. Half fill the entire length of the horizontal can with a barely moistened mixture of half sand/half soil. A little peat can be mixed in to help retain moisture and lighten the mixture somewhat. These trash can arrangements have proven very acceptable to female iguanas and can be used either indoors or out.

Prehensile-tailed Giant Skinks

Description: The prehensile-tailed skink, *Corucia zebrata,* is a big (to 2.5 feet [73.7 cm]), heavy-bodied lizard with a long, slender, strongly prehensile tail that is of somewhat greater length than the combined total of the head and body. It is a member of the subfamily Tiliquinae. The alternate name used by pet distributors is "monkey-tailed skink." Although we have kept and bred this species, we have found them far less "personable" than many others

The monkey-tailed skink, Corucia zebrata, *is the largest of the skinks and is of arboreal habits.*

of the tiliquines. The prehensile-tailed skinks offered in the pet trade are, in all but rare instances, wild-collected, imported adults.

In coloration *Corucia* is mostly olive and gray. The head of some specimens has an attractive yellow flush. Although the specific name of zebrata refers to banding, if bands are present they are often discontinuous and irregular. An irregular dark blotching is more common.

Although they can become accustomed to handling, be cautioned—their jaws are *immensely* powerful. You do not want to be bitten by one! Also, be aware that some specimens (even captive-born babies) are more aggressive than others. We have had specimens leap with widely opened jaws at an approaching hand.

A monotypic genus endemic to the Solomon Islands, *C. zebrata* is crepuscular and nocturnal in most activities, but has been seen active by day in densely shaded areas or during cloudy weather.

Keeping: The large outside cages in which we kept our specimens were situated beneath shade trees in our artificial Florida "rain forest." There the humidity was always high and on the rare occasion when artificial heat was necessary, it was supplied by a heat tape inside the suspended hollow log homes of the skinks. The cage in which they lived and bred was constructed of heavy ½ inch × 1 inch (13 × 25 mm) welded wire. It was a walk-in cage that measured 4 feet (122 cm) in width by 8 feet × 8 feet (244 cm × 244 cm) in length and height. Several hollowed logs were suspended from the top, leaving only space enough for the lizards to sit on top of them if they chose. The logs were accessed by the lizards by either climbing upright logs or by climbing up the sides of the cage. (Easily accessed cockatiel or parrot nesting boxes with a sufficiently enlarged entrance hole will also be readily accepted by the lizards.) An elevated water dish (a shallow, easily sterilized heavy plastic birdbath) was placed at a front corner of the cage. The lizards would climb down the wire to this when thirsty during the dry season, but drank copiously from rain pooling on their logs during our rainy season. These skinks easily withstood the summer temperatures in the high 90s°F (36–37.2°C) and their heat tape was activated when temperatures dropped to below 46°F (7.8°C). Had we maintained them indoors we would not have allowed the temperature to drop below 65°F (18°C). We have found that animals kept in naturalistic set-ups outdoors are more tolerant of existing extremes than those maintained inside.

Corucia is primarily herbivorous in the wild. Its main dietary items are the leaves of the climbing philodendron-like vines of the genus *Epipremnum.* These vines are considered toxic for many other creatures. The species of this plant genus most familiar to both American and European hobbyists is the common hanging-basket plant, *E. aureum,* better known as either *Pothos* or *Scindapsis.* If you supply greenhouse-grown pothos to your *Corucia,* be sure that you have sprinkled them enough to wash off any insecticides. (However, unless you are certain that systemic fungicides and insecticides have not been used by horticulturists, it is better not to provide your lizards houseplants as food items.)

Captive skinks thrive on a diet of diced fruit and vegetables and an occasional snail. The benefits, or potential harm, of animal protein in the diet of this species has not been fully explored. We feel that if animal protein is given at all, it should be only in minuscule amounts.

Corucia kept colonially develop a hierarchy. The introduction of a new adult specimen to a peacefully coexisting group will cause disorder and occasional fighting until the new hierarchy has been established. Be sure to provide sufficient separate areas of seclusion for all specimens.

Breeding: The *Corucia* that we have kept have been biennial breeders. They may be sexed by general appearance—the males have blockier heads, heavier jaws, and more slender bodies than the females. Sexing on younger specimens—those four months or older—can be done by manually everting the hemipenes, a process that requires two people. One person holds the lizard upside down while the other lifts the flap of skin covering the cloacal opening and then uses pressure in a rolling motion from the tail base toward the cloaca.

Females give birth to a single, proportionately *huge* baby, or, rarely, a set of slightly smaller twins. The neonates are readily accepted

If handled frequently when a baby many savanna monitors, Varanus exanthematicus, tame well and will remain tractable throughout their life.

into the existing colony. We never found it necessary to remove either the gravid females or the babies, although other hobbyists have found it necessary to separate their gravid females. Maternal (and colonial) protection of the neonates is marked. As parturition approaches, the gravid females become positively pugnacious toward human intrusion and short tempers are manifested by most, if not all, specimens in the colony after parturition. Fast-growing young and gravid females need much more frequent vitamin D_3 and calcium supplements than would be otherwise necessary.

Savanna Monitors

Description: The African savanna monitor, *V. exanthematicus,* is immensely popular in the pet trade. It is a grayish species with darker and lighter markings and much enlarged, roughened nuchal (nape) scales. The dorsal markings of juveniles often take the form of crossbands of light-centered dark ocelli. Juveniles (and especially hatchlings) also often have lines, "squiggles," or ocellar borders of red or russet. Most prominent on some hatchlings, even when present this color fades quickly with growth and is less apparent when the lizards are cool (or otherwise stressed) than when they are maintained at their optimum temperatures and conditions. Thus, when properly kept, some hatchling specimens of the savanna monitor can be very attractive. The body color of all, whether or not the red is present, will be lighter and prettier when the lizards are suitably warm and unstressed.

The savanna monitor is a proportionately stocky, dry land species. It commonly attains a length of about five feet (1.52 m) and some specimens may near six feet (1.83 m).

Frightened specimens huff and puff and inflate their body and throat, turn sideways to the perceived threat and lash with their tail. Savanna monitors employ several other defensive ploys. They rake with their claws, void their odoriferous cloacal contents, and play dead. While the tail-lashing may be used by even well-acclimated captives if they are startled, the latter two ploys are seldom used by tame (or even half-tame) monitors.

Keeping: Obviously, a lizard of this size will need a savanna-type cage at least 6 × 6 × 10 square feet

(1.83 m × 1.83 m × 3.05 m); a room-sized cage would be much better. These lizards are ready feeders and with advanced age captive savanna monitors can become grossly obese. Limit food intake to keep your lizard's weight within acceptable parameters. Unfortunately, there has been no monitor size/weight chart produced; your intuition will necessarily be your guide.

Breeding: Although monitors of many kinds are considered difficult to breed, both private hobbyists and zoological gardens have succeeded with savanna monitors a few times. Like all other monitors, savannas can be difficult-to-impossible to sex from external characteristics. Everting the hemipenes by using a rolling pressure on the base of the tail toward the cloaca may work. Some males evert their hemipenes briefly after defecation, but timing your observation may be difficult. (See the breeding section on the green iguana, pages 65–67 for monitor breeding guidelines.)

Clutches of, or nearing as many as, 50 eggs laid in a burrow excavated by the female have been recorded. Most clutches seem half that size, or fewer. Babies are seven to eight inches (17.8 cm–20.3 cm) when they hatch.

Nile Monitors

Description: The bad-tempered Nile monitor is a common pet trade species, both in Europe and the

Because they are inexpensive when babies, Nile monitors are often purchased as pets. Many do not tame well and a 6-foot-long (1.8-m) adult can be difficult (even dangerous!) to handle.

United States. As a baby, its defensive ploys seem harmless enough, but as the lizard grows, the tail-lashing, the biting, and the raking with the claws become proportionately more determined and painful. Although time and frequent gentle handling (this means three times a day) may quiet them somewhat, Nile monitors cannot be considered pets by any means.

The color of the Nile monitor, *V. niloticus,* is blackish with yellow spots forming crossbands. Only two subspecies—*niloticus* and *ornatus*—are recognized by American taxonomists. *Ornatus* is a particularly pretty form. Its large, rounded yellow spots are contained in broad, otherwise unmarked, black bands. These contrast strongly with the buffered black of the rest of the body. The yellow spots lengthen into short crossbars posteriorly and are complete bands

The bright colors of a hatchling Dumeril's monitor, Varanus dumerilii, *soon dull and adults are often nervous captives.*

on the tail. The *niloticus* form is more variable, but the yellow spots or bards are not contained within a contrasting black band. Between the yellow, the body may vary from solid black to black that is well peppered with the tiniest of yellowish spots. One to four U-shaped yellow markings are usually present on the rear of the head and the nape.

The vast majority of the Nile monitors available in the pet trade are babies collected from the wild. If larger than a hatchling when collected, there is probably no species of monitor harder to tame.

Keeping: In captivity, Nile monitors need large cages, with a young specimen being kept easily in a 40-gallon (151 L) "long" savanna tank. Adult specimens will be cramped in a cage 6 feet × 6 feet × 10 feet (1.83 m × 1.83 m × 3.05 m) and would be better off in one that is room-sized.

Although most adults are smaller, Nile monitors can attain a length of more than 6.5 feet (196 cm). The babies, which are quite arboreal, feed on insects and other arthropods, carrion, smaller lizards, nestling rodents, or whatever else they can ferret out. They use both visual and chemical cues when hunting. Their long snout serves them in good stead, allowing them to grasp insects in narrow spaces.

With growth, the skull becomes heavier and the snout less attenuate. This allows the lizard to easily overpower the mollusk, crustacean, fish, and mammalian diet that it now utilizes. The Nile monitor is especially fond of the eggs of crocodiles. With increased size, the Nile monitor becomes less arboreal, turning instead to terrestrial and aquatic habitats. It is a powerful swimmer.

Breeding: Nile monitors are rarely bred in captivity. Female Nile monitors will dig a deep nesting chamber in moist (*not* wet) earth. They may do so more readily if the earth is contained in a barrel or is secluded behind some sort of opaque barrier that echoes their choice in the wild of a termite mound. The female will have to be comfortable and unstressed to nest. Unless conditions are conducive to nesting, the female Nile monitor may just scatter her eggs on the floor of her cage or, worse yet, retain them until egg solidification or adherence occur, either/both of which require surgical intervention.

Nile monitors lay large clutches. More than 15 eggs are normally laid, and clutches of over 50 eggs have been recorded. In nature, the eggs may take the better part of a year to incubate. Incubation in captivity may take somewhat less than half that expected in the wild.

If fed adequately and kept suitably warm, hatchlings will grow quickly. A sizable water container—one large enough for this water-loving lizard to climb in and soak/submerge—should be provided for this species.

As with many large lizards, if handled gently and frequently when a baby, black and white tegus, Tupinambis merianae, *may remain tame as adults.*

Tegus

Description: Tegus are alert South American lizards that are well adapted to extremes of weather and temperature. When disturbed, they run bipedally. Two genera are found in captivity: *Callopistes,* the dwarf tegus, and *Tupinambis,* the larger tegus.

The Argentine red tegu, Tupinambis rufescens, *is adult at a hefty 4 feet (1.2 m) in length. Although juveniles can climb, this species is predominantly terrestrial.*

Keeping: Captives appreciate a well-illuminated daytime basking area that approaches a surface temperature of 100°F (38°C) and, as long as the lizards can readily retreat from the area of intense heat when necessary, the surface temperature of the basking spot can even be allowed to near the 105°F (40.6°C) mark. The remainder of the cage or terrarium should be in the 85 to 90°F (29–32.2°C) range. Nighttime temperatures can be allowed to drop rather radically. Southernmost and high altitude specimens of both genera overwinter by hibernation.

Tegus will eat almost anything, both in nature and in captivity. Rodents, insects, nestling birds, some prepared foods, and some vegetation will be accepted. They

seem to prefer succulent fruit over leafy vegetables.

Due to their large adult size, tegus require big caging facilities. Many persons allow a tame tegu the run of a room. In the hotter southerly climes, tegus are often kept in screened rooms or pool areas. If the screen extends to the ground, reinforce it to assure that your lizard will be restrained. Traditional outside lizard pens will work for tegus with one consideration: because these are adept climbers and can jump upwards, a full cage cover is important.

Tegus, *Tupinambis* sp.

Description: Tupinambis are habitat generalists, occupying a variety of forest-to-savanna habitats but excluding deserts. The lizards are

Red tegu babies grow to adults of more than 4 feet (1.3 m) in a few years. If handled regularly (i.e., daily), they may remain tractable—a boon for both them and their owners.

often found near water, and preferentially spend long periods of time soaking in water. They may also defecate in their water dish, thus water quality must be closely monitored.

Tupinambis have both femoral and preanal pores. Males may be identified by the presence of a small postanal spur on each side of the tail base. These are composed of (usually) three barely protruding ventrolateral scales. Although small, the spurs are easily visible if the lizard is in hand.

Black and Gold Tegus, *T. teguixin*

Description: Because imported specimens have remained readily available and inexpensive, the black and gold tegus, *T. teguixin*, have served as the introductory species of this lizard genus for many hobbyists; however, ready availability seldom means that a lizard is well adapted to captivity. When obtained as subadults or adults, these large (to three feet [91 cm]) lizards will scratch, bite, whip with their tails, and void excrement on their handler. Those that are obtained young and handled frequently and carefully can become quite tractable. The black and gold tegu may hibernate, or at least become intermittently dormant in cooler areas.

Keeping: See discussion of keeping Tegus, page 74.

Breeding: Black and gold tegus are seldom bred in captivity. Little is known about the procedures necessary to cycle these common lizards for breeding.

Black and White Tegus and Red Tegus

Description: The black and white, *T. merianae,* and the red tegu, *T. rufesceus,* hibernate throughout their range.

Of the tegus, it is the black and white (colored as its name suggests) and the red (black with extensive markings of pale to bright red) that are the most cold tolerant. Since it is these two that occur the farthest south (the most temperate regions) in the range of the genus, this tolerance is understandable.

Keeping: For black and white tegus and red tegus kept in outdoor enclosures, preparations for hibernation—cessation of feeding, digging, and perhaps filling a hibernaculum with leaves, straw, and other such materials—begin while the weather is still warm. Hibernation lengths of 65 days (red tegu) and 100 days (black and white) have been reported by breeders. A hibernation temperature of 48–54°F (8.9–12°C) is suggested.

Breeding: Once they emerge from hibernation, males court the females, breeding occurs, and eggs are deposited in a burrow prepared by the female. Some females line the burrow with straw, leaves or other provided materials, and occupy the burrow, on top of the eggs until they hatch. For artificial incubation of the eggs of the black and gold tegu (obtained from gravid, imported females), an incubation temperature of 83 to 86°F (28–30°C) will result in hatching from approximately 120 to more than 170 days, a much longer incubation duration than is known for other more temperate tegu species. (This lengthy incubation period is difficult to explain; of all of the tegus, the climatic conditions at the latitude where the black and gold tegu occurs seem the most equable for rapid incubation. Perhaps embryonic development temporarily ceases during the dry season. Such a diapause is well documented in other reptiles.)

Chapter Nine
The Desert Terrarium

Before discussing the desert lizard species, a word about the desert terrarium is in order.

Many terrestrial and saxicolous (rock-dwelling) lizard species are desert dwellers. The desert habitat cage can be large or small, complex or simple, depending on your wallet and the sizes and activity patterns of your specimens.

Although you may be cautioned against the use of sand as a substrate (citing intestinal impactions if it is ingested by the lizard inhabitants), in more than 40 years of lizard keeping we have *never* lost a single specimen to impaction. However, we do suggest that you avoid using sharp-sided silica aquarium gravel; if accidentally ingested by your specimens it could be of more potential danger than the finer builder's sand. If the possibility of sand-related problems does worry you, consider using smooth, variably-sized river rocks.

The depth of the substrate can vary. If only a half-inch (12.7 mm) layer, your tank will, of course, be lighter and easier to move and handle. If a thick layer of substrate is used, you will be able to better maintain the barely dampened bottom layer and the dry top layer preferred by some desert lizard species. To moisten the bottom layers only, push a piece of PVC or other pipe to the bottom of the tank. Slowly pour a little water through the pipe. Capillary action will carry the water along the bottom layers of sand, providing the desired moisture gradient.

Rock ledges and caves, individual basking rocks, potted aridland plants, corkbark hiding areas, and opuntia cactus skeletons can be provided both for decoration and the psychological well-being of your specimen(s). Since most desert-dwelling reptiles are adapted to low humidity, to prevent condensation and promote air exchange, the top of your desert terrarium should be of screen.

Like most other habitats, deserts are found at all elevations and desert temperature range may vary widely. Research the area of origin for your lizard, so you can provide the temperature range and cycling it needs.

Many lizard species, such as this Texas whiptail, Aspidoscelis gularis, *thrive in desert terraria.*

Horned Lizards, Swifts, and Relatives

Description: The phrynosomatines, consisting of about ten genera of New World lizards, is one of the recent "spinoffs" from the family Iguanidae. The lizards in this family share many characteristics, but it is their nasal physiology that firmly unites them. These lizards are of two quite distinct body shapes: There are the horned lizards of the genus *Phrynosoma*, all rather slow, basically short, squat, and thorny, and the swifts (or spiny lizards), and their relatives (*Sceloporus* and related genera). All of these latter, called "scelops or sceloporines," are slender, fast moving, and comparatively streamlined. The eardrum or tympanum may or may not be exposed. Those species not having exposed tympani are often referred to as earless lizards.

Many members of this family are popular with hobbyists. Indeed, some, such as the fence swifts and horned lizards, are among the first lizards noticed and kept by young enthusiasts.

Keeping: Terrarium size should be determined by the size, normal activity patterns, and numbers of lizards to be kept within. One or two horned lizards (not suggested captive species) may be maintained for a few days in a terrarium with a floorspace of 12 inches × 30 inches (30.5 cm × 76 cm) or larger. These terrestrial lizards will require no climbing props or other such furniture, but might appreciate piles of flat rocks. A terrarium of similar size can be used for tree and side-blotched lizards, but both of these closely allied genera will readily utilize all manner of climbing props. Small swifts (spiny lizards) are also candidates for terraria of this size, again with either or both rockpiles or limbs for climbing. If several specimens are to be maintained, use a larger terrarium. A substrate of sand is ideal.

Although adult males of many of the phrynosomatid lizards are less overtly aggressive to others of their sex than males of other groupings, low-level stress can and usually does occur. Over a period of time this can be every bit as harmfully overwhelming to subordinate lizards as overt aggression. Therefore, we suggest that no more than a single male be kept to each enclosure, but feel that several compatible females can be kept with each male.

Most of these lizards enjoy dry facilities, hot (to 105–110°F, 40.6–43°C), illuminated basking areas, and low relative cage humidity. The emerald swift, a Latin American species, the range of which extends well up into cloud forest clearings, can withstand higher relative humidity than desert-dwelling forms.

The larger swifts and rock lizards are fast and active climbers. A pair or trio may be maintained in a terrarium with a floor space of 12 inches × 48 inches (30.5 cm × 122 cm) or larger. We prefer 18 inches × 48 inches (45.7 cm × 122 cm). These lizards will climb on both rocks and tank-length sections of limbs of no less than the diameter of their body.

The horned lizards and many of the fine-scaled desert forms (zebra-tailed and earless lizards) are specialist feeders on specific ant types, and are difficult if not impossible to keep in captivity. Many of the horned lizards are now protected by law.

Although horned lizards may continue to be active after nightfall, most members of this family are primarily diurnal. We have watched a Texas horned lizard actively feeding at an anthill in light so dim that we used a flashlight.

The beautiful emerald swift, a tropical American montane species, has also proven difficult to maintain in captivity. This has been especially true in very warm areas of the United States. Please read the species account for this lizard carefully (see page 82).

Breeding: Unfortunately, few American enthusiasts attempt to breed any but the petrosaurs or rock lizards. Perhaps this is because wild-caught specimens of most species are inexpensive and readily available to American hobbyists. European hobbyists, who find it somewhat more difficult to acquire these specimens and for whom many of the species are considerably more expensive, have a much better track record in captive breeding.

In most cases, a period of from 60 to 90 days of winter dormancy (50–56°F, 10–13°C) seems necessary to cycle the temperate species reproductively. In contrast, some tropical species may require only slightly reduced nighttime temperatures, reduced photoperiod, and a period of reduced relative humidity to attain sexual receptiveness.

Among the lizards in this group are both live-bearing and egg-laying species. The eggs of some have proven a little difficult to hatch. We suggest an incubation temperature range of 84 to 87°F (28.9–30.6°C), and that only as much humidity be provided as is necessary to keep the eggs from seriously dehydrating. Dimpling, or even partial collapse of an egg, does not necessarily indicate embryo death, and overhydrating eggs (especially eggs of desert lizards) may be more detrimental to a developing embryo than a slight underhydration would be.

Rock Lizards

Description: A bitypic, oviparous lizard genus, *Petrosaurus* is represented in the United States (California) and northern Baja by *P. mearnsi* and on the southern Baja by two subspecies of *P. thalassinus*. Of the two, *P. thalassinus* is the larger, the more colorful, very much more in demand, and the only of the two to be bred in captivity.

Both members of this genus are flattened and have a spraddle-legged stance that, despite looking awkward, carries them swiftly and surely over the rock faces of their habitats. They seem to move horizontally or perpendicularly, skittering along, clinging to either upper or inverted surfaces with equal facility.

P. mearnsi is often called the banded rock lizard and *P. thalassinus* the Baja rock lizard.

Although no longer legally imported for the pet trade, there is sufficient captive breeding stock of the Baja rock lizard to ensure the occasional appearance of captive hatched babies at specialist dealers.

Keeping: Babies can be kept in 15- to 20-gallon (56.8 L–75.7 L) terraria, but for a trio of the 15-inch-long (38 cm) adults we suggest a 55- to 75-gallon (208 L–284 L) (floor size 12 inches × 48 inches to 18 inches × 48 inches, 30.5 cm × 122 cm to 45.7 cm × 122 cm) terrarium. A sand substrate and firmly stacked (immovable) rocks are suggested.

The Baja rock lizard is actually quite variably colored with males being larger and brighter than females and having a heavy tail base. Although rock lizards have rather small femoral pores, those of the males, especially when in breeding readiness, are proportionately larger than those of the female. The prettiest of the rock lizards is *P. t. thalassinus,* the race found at the southernmost regions of the Baja Peninsula.

The color of the Baja rock lizard is complex and difficult to describe. Dorsally, the head, anterior body, and tail are blue. Three to four

The beautifully colored and aptly named Baja rock lizard, Petrosaurus thalassinus, *prefers a rocky habitat.*

black bands, the first on the nape, the last about midbody, are present. The bands are edged posteriorly with yellow (or in gravid females, with orange). The rump is orangish. Posterior to the last black band the dorsal color is duller, but has either a bluish or an orangish wash and obscure darker banding is usually visible. The orbits of both sexes are often a vivid orange, and gravid females develop a bright orange throat and snout. The colors, pretty at all times, become vibrantly brilliant with suitable body warmth and ultraviolet exposure.

Insects, blossoms (and in captivity, fruit-honey gecko mixture) are eagerly consumed. These are powerful lizards that are capable of overpowering and consuming sizable insects. If kept dry and warm these lizards will thrive as captives. We recommend a large terrarium for this species.

Breeding: In nature, reproductive cycling is triggered by lengthening springtime photoperiods, rising temperatures, and elevated relative humidity. A clutch contains up to a dozen fairly large eggs. Eggs incubate best in "low humidity" conditions at a temperature of 85–88°F (29–31°C).

American Horned Lizards

There are probably no lizards anywhere in the world more easily recognized by non-enthusiasts than the New World horned lizards (genus *Phrynosoma*). To most persons who encounter them, the horned lizards are "horny toads." These spiny lizards are paralleled in spiny-ness only by Australia's thorny devil or moloch. However, amongst the horny toads are some rarely seen forms which are nearly lacking in spines. No less spectacular, they are nonetheless of very different appearance. The genus is best represented in the American southwest and northern Mexico, but one species ranges northward to southern British Columbia and Alberta, Canada. Another occurs as far southward as the Central American country of Guatemala.

The majority of these lizards feed largely on ants in the wild. Many are reluctant to change this dietary preference, and although they may feed on other insects in captivity, decline and die.

Males have thicker tail bases and much larger femoral pores than females.

Although most species are egg layers, some high altitude forms give birth to living young.

None of the horned lizards are easily kept. We feel they are best left in the wild.

American Spiny Lizards (also called Swifts and Fence Lizards)

Description: Despite the efforts to term members of this genus "spiny lizards," the older names of "swift" and "fence lizard," both apropos, continue to be regularly used.

Of the 75 plus species of *Sceloporus,* a scant handful is seen in the pet trade. These lizards are much more in demand in Europe than in the United States. Among the members are both oviparous and ovoviviparous species. The largest species is near 14 inches (35.6 cm) in overall length while the smallest species are barely a third that size.

Males are often more brilliantly colored both dorsally and ventrally than females. The males of most species have bilateral patches of blue (rose on some species) on

each side of their belly. Many also have a dark throat. Besides these differences, males also have thicker tail-bases and larger femoral pores than the females.

Within the United States alone there are 16 species, of which some are among the largest and others among the smallest of the genus. Although among the United States species there are none that attain the brilliance of the ovoviviparous, Latin American emerald swift, *S. malachiticus,* the granite spiny lizard, *Sceloporus orcutti,* is considered one of the most beautiful of our native lizard species. Males attain a total length of 10.5 inches (26.7 cm), of which some 4.5 inches (11.4 cm) is snout-vent length. Females are somewhat smaller.

Light phase adult male *S. orcutti* may vary in ground color from copper to charcoal. A dark wedge, often

The black spot above the armpit will help identify the rose-bellied lizard, Sceloporus variabilis. *Although the majority of the spiny lizards or swifts are typified by blue belly patches, males of the rose-bellied lizard,* Sceloporus variabilis, *have pink belly patches.*

The purple-backed phase of the granite spiny lizard, Sceloporus orcutti, *is one of the prettiest examples of this large genus.*

obscured in darker males, is present on each shoulder. Dorsally, scales are marked with black, turquoise, and yellow-green. The entire venter and throat are brilliant blue. Light phase males often have a broad stripe of intense purple for the entire length of the dorsum. Females tend more toward a coppery ground color, are often prominently banded, and have the purple dorsal area less well defined. The venter is whitish or faintly washed with blue. Juveniles are prominently crossbanded.

The scales of the neck, sides, posterior dorsum, and tail are heavily keeled and spinose. Scales of the anterior dorsum are rounded posteriorly and decidedly less keeled and spinose.

The granite spiny's common name aptly describes its preferred habitat. Jumbles of granite boulders, cliff faces, and escarpments are the preferred habitat over much of its range. It is associated in the north with chaparral, pines, mesquite, and palms, and in the south with these and thorn forests. *Orcutti* occurs in suitable habitat below a 7,000 foot (2,134 m) elevation. Its actual distribution is spotty.

Keeping: Scelops are active, alert lizards that should be provided comparatively large terraria.

Because the various species occupy such diverse habitats, the captive care necessary can also be variable. As an example, the little striped bunch-grass lizard, *S. scalaris* of southwest New Mexico, southeast Arizona, and adjacent Mexico occurs at cool elevations of up to 10,000 feet (3,048 m) and requires a cool terrarium with a hotspot, while the big, widely distributed desert spiny lizard, *S. magister,* also of the southwest United States and northern Mexico, may be found in the heat of semiarid habitats, virtually at sea level.

S. orcutti seems to be a hardy captive, and feeds avidly upon mealworms, crickets, grubs, and locusts. It also eats occasional dandelion blossoms. If kept indoors, both full-spectrum lighting and superwarmed

The taxonomic status of this taxon, the northern prairie lizard, Sceloporus undulatus garmani, *is now in question.*

Incubation temperatures of from 82 to 89°F (27.8–31.7°C) seem to suffice. We generally strive for temperatures midway between these extremes.

The common spiny lizard, *S. undulatus,* and its relatives are widely distributed in the United States. In the East it is a lizard of the pine oak woodlands and is particularly common in clearings where there are many fallen trees and even on the fence rails that surround pastures. It is not an uncommon species amidst the debris of rural homesteads.

Description: The eastern forms have posteriorly directed, dark, wavy dorsal chevrons. Males are less strongly patterned than females and have brilliant turquoise, greenish-blue, or rich-blue ventral patches and throat patch. These are bordered on the inside edges with black. If the females have any blue ventrally, it is very much reduced and not bordered with darker pigment. A dark stripe is present on the rear of the thigh.

Many small western species of spiny lizards are known as prairie or plateau lizards. Most are very strongly marked with longitudinal bands rather than crossbars. The males, often having chestnut lateral areas striped with straw-yellow, are the more richly colored.

At 14.25 inches (36 cm), *S. cyanogenys,* the blue spiny lizard, is the largest of the United States spiny lizards.

basking areas need to be provided. A low relative humidity situation seems best. If kept outdoors, the enclosure must be in full sun, offer protection from heavy rains, and be well drained. Drainage is especially important in humid areas. Excess moisture will produce a difficult-to-cure bacterial dermatitus or "blister disease," which will eventually be fatal to the affected lizards.

Breeding: This is an oviparous species. Each clutch contains from 6 to 15 eggs. Deposition occurs in early or midsummer. A large female kept by us laid 11 parchment-shelled eggs in late June. Incubation lasted for 57 days at a variable (room) temperature. The hatchlings consumed small crickets within a day of hatching.

Both nighttime cooling and natural photoperiod are probably necessary to induce breeding and the production of viable eggs.

The emerald swift, Sceloporus malachiticus, *of Mexico and Central America is not always easily acclimated.*

Description: The black collar against a steel-blue to rather bright blue ground combine to make a beautiful lizard. This, too, is a rock-dwelling species of southern Texas and adjacent Mexico. It is easily confused with the slightly smaller crevice spiny lizard, *S. poinsetti,* a species from slightly farther west in Texas and Mexico. The tail of the blue spiny lizard is not prominently banded, while that of the crevice spiny lizard is. Most crevice spiny lizards are also grayer than the blue spiny lizard, but there is much variability. Both of these species bear live young.

Although the emerald (or malachite) swift, *S. malachiticus,* has become a mainstay in the pet industry, it is also one of the more difficult species to maintain for long periods. This is a high elevation, live-bearing species from Latin America. We have frequently encountered them on rocks and fallen trees in cloud forests from Mexico to Central America.

Description: The males are brilliant green (some specimens have dark markings) both dorsally and laterally and have bright blue ventral patches that are edged on the inner edge with black, and orange and blue throats. The females are smaller, often with olive overtones, with well-defined darker markings dorsally. The neonates are duller yet. Males attain a length of more than seven inches (17.8 cm). Besides insects, emerald swifts will eat blossoms and some sweet fruits. Emerald swifts enjoy cooler temperatures daytimes of 72–80°F (22–27°C) with a well-illuminated, warmer basking area. A temperature of up to 94°F (34°C) can be allowed beneath the basking light. Nighttime temperatures can be allowed to drop to the high 60s°F (20°C). Those kept in large cages with a wide variety of climbing, hiding, and "peering" sites seem to do better that those in smaller cages.

Emerald swifts are often heavily parasitized. Fecal smears should be prepared and checked by a knowledgeable veterinarian and an appropriate pesticide administered if necessary.

There are several additional species of spiny lizards that occasionally enter the pet market. Most respond well to the one or the other of the regimens of care suggested here. Correct identification of the species involved may be difficult,

so experiment and change husbandry procedures as necessary. Most spiny lizards are hardy and enjoyable additions to a collection.

Tree Lizards and Side-blotched Lizards

Several species of the genera Urosaurus (tree lizards) and Uta (side-blotched lizards) are often seen in the pet trade. All are small. Reproductively active males of some species and populations are magnificently colored. Colors fade when the breeding season ends and when the lizards are frightened. In America the lizards of these genera are more eagerly sought as a food source for hatchling milk snakes than for the terrarium qualities of the lizards themselves. This is unfortunate, for, with reasonable care, both the side-blotched and the tree lizards can be both hardy and long-lived. These lizards feed upon small insects and other arthropods, most of which are found in bark crevices or dead wood in the trees, or among the rocks where the lizards abound.

Despite these species being commonly seen in the American pet trade, we are unaware of any hobbyist efforts to breed them.

Tree lizards, Urosaurus ornatus *(top), and the side-blotched lizard,* Uta stansburiana *(bottom), are rather closely related.*

All comments pertaining to the reproduction of egg-laying spiny lizards (swifts) pertain here.

Leopard Geckos and Relatives

There are few reptile enthusiasts who do not immediately recognize members of this grouping. It is undoubtedly the leopard gecko, *Eublepharis macularius,* which is the most familiar, for these alert and hardy lizards are now both commercially and privately captive bred annually by the tens of thousands. The big African fat-tailed gecko, *Hemitheconyx caudicinctus,* is almost as familiar. Still not as popular but becoming more common are the various banded geckos of the North and Middle American genus *Coleonyx* and the larger Latin American species *C. elegans* and *C. mitratus.*

A species seldom seen until mid-1996 has recently become available in the American pet trade—the Vietnam leopard gecko, *Goniurosaurus lichtenfelderi* ssp. Virtually nothing is known about the captive husbandry of this latter species but, hopefully, this paucity will soon be replaced with knowledge.

Of significance to conservation-minded hobbyists is the fact that most available specimens of the two most popular eublepharines—the leopard and the fat-tailed geckos—are captive-bred offspring. This means that even though these geckos are sold by the thousands in the pet

Small though it may be, the Texas banded gecko, Coleonyx brevis, is a beautiful relative of the leopard gecko.

trade, their popularity places a minimal drain on the wild populations.

Description: Most of the commonly seen eublepharine geckos are desert and dry savanna/thornbrush dwellers. All have well-developed, fully functional eyelids and no toepads. The tails of some are proportionately slender, those of others, heavy. All eublepharines have the caudal (tail) scales arranged in distinct whorls. The tails of all are easily broken but those of the slender-tailed species are especially so, and, as with other lizards, the regenerated tail differs from the original in shape and color. Rather than being rigidly calcified, the eggs of the eublepharine geckos have soft, somewhat pliable shells.

Since they are rather slow-moving and confiding, most eublepharines can be moved by shepherding them into the palm of one hand with the other, then cupping them with the free hand to prevent them from falling.

Keeping: As a group, eublepharine geckos are found in both North and Latin America, Asia, and tropical Africa. Wild eublepharines feed on insects and other invertebrates. Some of the larger species are capable of overpowering and eating small nestlings of ground-nesting birds and rodents. Similar diets are accepted by captives. These geckos adapt well to a captive diet of crickets, common and giant mealworms, a very few waxworms (these have an unhealthy calcium/phosphorus ratio), butterworms, spiders, and other commonly available arthropods. Newly born (pinky) mice are also eagerly accepted by many, if not most of the larger geckos. Offer a varied diet when possible. Although eublepharines are capable of eating comparatively large prey items, food offered should be kept within reason. If you're lucky enough to have access to an insecticide-free yard or garden, an even more variable diet can be offered to your lizards. Not only are sowbugs and hairless caterpillars a welcome change, but, due to their more varied diet, wild insects generally contain more nutrition than domestically raised ones. Occasionally dust the insects with a calcium/multi-vitamin additive that is high in D_3 before feeding them to your geckos. Supplemental calcium and vitamin D_3 is especially important to gravid females or for rapidly growing juveniles.

Most wild-caught eublepharine geckos have internal parasites. Testing and any needed treatment should be done by your reptile veterinarian.

Adult male eublepharine geckos are highly territorial and skirmishes will eventually occur if two males are housed together. The sparring will become more severe as the geckos settle in (one male will *have* to assert dominance) and will worsen even more at breeding time. Vocalizations, feints, and actual attacks may occur. Females are more compatible (or at least, less agonistic) than males and, usually, several may be kept with a single male. However, occasionally a female will become aggressive toward one or more of her cagemates and you will have to adjust her (your) caging accordingly. Subordinate eublepharine geckos, whether male or female, should be

Holodactylus africanus is known as the African clawed gecko. It is a small eublepharine gecko that seems comfortable only after darkness has fallen.

removed and placed in a more agreeable environment. If left in place, a subordinate gecko may either refuse food or its health will otherwise deteriorate due to stress.

Description: *C. elegans* ssp. (southern Mexico, northern Guatemala and Belize) and *C. mitratus* (El Salvador and Honduras to Panama) are two of the larger members of this genus. Both have tuberculate dorsal skin. In most external appearances these two species greatly resemble each other. The most significant external difference between these two *Coleonyx* are in the head patterns. The nuchal bridle of *C. elegans* is proportionately narrow, with the ends involving the uppermost portion of the eyes. The nuchal bridle of *C. mitratus* is wider with the ends involving most of the eye. Also, hatchlings of *C. mitratus* have the prominent bark tail rings broken subcaudally. The tail rings of *C. elegans* are entire.

Unlike their congeners, all denizens of open or rocky desert and semidesert and associated cliffs and escarpments, *C. elegans* and *C. mitratus* inhabit dry open forest, thornscrub and seasonally wet secondary forest. Both species are variable in coloration and pattern. In fact, in certain areas of the Yucatan Peninsula, *C. e. elegans* occurs in both a banded and a striped morph.

Leopard Geckos

Although subspecies are known, because of generations of captivity-

The leopard gecko, Eublepharis macularis, *an Asiatic species, is now bred in so many designer colors (a high yellow [top] and a leucistic [bottom] are pictured here) that the original wild phase is all but forgotten.*

induced intergradation, it would be almost impossible to assign a subspecies to the leopard geckos now being produced in American breeding programs. Many, having originated from the vicinity of Quetta, West Pakistan, would be *E. macularius montanus. E. m. fasciolatus* of Pakistan's coastal lowlands and adjacent India, is also imported.

Leopard geckos are a hardy, long-lived species. Captive records of 15 to 22 years are not uncommon.

The distinctive black and yellow bands of the juveniles tend to break into a pattern of spots and reticulations as the lizards mature. Breeders strive to produce aberrant colors, working particularly for a reduction of black pigment. Leucistic examples, inordinately dark specimens, and other color aberrancies are known.

Keeping: Because of their inactivity, terraria for leopard geckos can be relatively small. A terrarium made from a ten-gallon (38 L) tank will house one male and three females without overcrowding. Use an inch or two (2.5–5.1 cm) of sand, finely ground oyster shell, small pebbles, or dry cypress mulch for substrate. Preformed caves, corkbark tubes, or curved pieces of pine bark all make good hiding areas for these nocturnal lizards. A low receptacle of clean water should always be present.

African Fat-tailed Geckos

Second among eublepharines only to the leopard gecko in recognition factor is the species called the African fat-tailed gecko, *Hemitheconyx caudicinctus.* Although there are actually two species in the genus, the Somalian *H. taylori,* is not known to be in captivity in America.

Description: Fully adult male fat-tailed geckos attain an overall length of more than eight inches (20 cm). Females are noticeably smaller.

This beautiful tropical west African gecko is an inhabitant of dry, rocky woodlands and savannas and their environs. Like all eublepharines save *Aeluroscalabotes, Hemitheconyx caudicinctus* is a terrestrial gecko that is adept at secluding itself beneath natural and man-made debris. It also seeks out deserted burrows of small mammals in which to hide.

Much of the field biology of this nocturnal gecko remains speculative. It does seem to be more active in the wet season than in the dry. In fact, the fat-tailed geckos may be largely inactive during the driest times of the year. In captivity, fat-tails remain active year round. Male fat-tails squeak and "click" when upset or involved in territorial disputes.

Fat-tailed geckos occur in several color phases. One, where the lizard is pleasingly and broadly banded in contrasting shades of tan and dark chocolate brown, is usually referred to as the common banded phase. A second phase, in which a white vertebral stripe of variable thickness is added to the banded pattern, is called the striped phase. Occasionally, on both banded and striped phases, the light areas are suffused with peach and the dark crossbands suffused with orange. The effect is startlingly beautiful and efforts are being made by private breeders to perpetuate and even enhance the color. Juveniles are much more brilliantly colored than the adults, being clad in bands of dark chocolate and yellow. Males can be distinguished from the females by their better-developed preanal pores and by the hemipenial bulges at the base of the tail.

Second in popularity among the eublepharine geckos, the African fat-tailed gecko, Hemitheconyx caudicinctus, *is large (to 8 inches [20 cm]) and heavy bodied. This is a striped normal phase.*

Keeping: Once only sporadically captive bred, African fat-tailed geckos are being produced today in large and ever-increasing numbers. Although they are considered by most hobbyists to be "not quite" as hardy and "not quite" as easy to breed as the leopard geckos, we have found the two virtually identical in all respects. Fat-tails prefer their terrarium conditions just a little more humid than leopard geckos. This may be provided with a substrate of bark nuggets, a medium that, in perpetually humid areas such as Florida, holds slightly more moisture than sand. In dry areas of the world, fat-tails can be provided with a suitably-sized receptacle of *barely* moistened, unmilled sphagnum moss into which they can crawl. Plastic refrigerator dishes for sandwiches are ideal. Some keepers keep these tightly covered, cutting an access hole in the top. Fat-tail geckos drink readily from low water dishes and avidly accept most types of insects and newly-born mice as prey.

The eggs of this lizard are typically eublepharine in that they have soft shells. Like the leopard geckos, the moisture content of the incubation medium must be neither too damp or too dry.

Breeding: Some eublepharines, like the leopard gecko, mature quickly and may attain sexual maturity in slightly less than a year. Adult eublepharines may be easily sexed by comparing the areas immediately anterior and posterior to the vent (anus). Males, especially those that are sexually active, can be distinguished from the females by their bulbous tail base (containing the hemipenes) and, on many but not all species, by a vaguely chevron-shaped arrangement of enlarged preanal pores. Females that are incubated at very high temperatures often have male-like preanal pores. Males of some eublepharine species are slightly larger than the females.

As with many other lizards, the sex of eublepharine geckos is determined by incubation temperature rather than genetically. This is referred to as "temperature-dependent sex determination" and commonly designated by the acronym "TDSD." To produce both sexes, incubation temperatures should range from 84 to 87°F (29–31°C). If cooler than 84°F (29°C), the sex ratio of the hatchlings will favor females; if warmer than 87°F (30.6°C), a preponderance of males will develop. If for some reason incubation temperatures drift upwards into the mid-90s°F (35°C), females are again produced, but many embryos will die in the egg. Excessively warm incubation temperatures may result in skeletal deformities or other aberrancies. Among these aberrancies, extraordinarily light colors (some bordering on a leucistic appearance) can occur.

Leopard and fat-tailed geckos are two of the easiest lizard species to breed. Usually, if the lizards are well fed they will breed—no preambles, no fumbling with husbandry manipulations. The better the lizards are fed, the more clutches they will have each season and the healthier the hatchlings will be.

However, though winter cooling may not be a mandatory prelude to successful breeding of many eublepharines, cooling and shortening the photoperiod may actually be best for the lizards, and some breeders feel that the typical winter temperature and photoperiod manipulations will measurably enhance your likelihood of success.

A healthy female eublepharine gecko should produce several clutches of two eggs each over the seven- or eight-month breeding season. Incubation duration varies somewhat with temperature, but will probably average about 55 days.

Being soft-shelled, eublepharine eggs are quite moisture-permeable, which makes the level of moisture in the incubation medium critical.

Collared and Leopard Lizards

Although native lizards are generally regarded boring by hobbyists and are ignored in the pet trade, a small number of our collared and leopard lizards appear each year at dealers and pet shops. This is understandable, for among these lizards are some of the most beautifully colored of any American squa-

The Malaysian cat gecko, Aleuroscalobotes felinus, *is the most divergent of the eublepharine geckos.*

mates. Both sexes are at their brightest during the breeding and egg deposition season, with the males being the brighter. When gravid, females of all species bear lateral bars or spots of orange.

Description: The two genera, *Crotaphytus* (collared lizards) and *Gambelia* (leopard lizards), of the family Iguanidae are easily differentiated. The collared lizards are big headed and squatty, the leopard lizards are narrow headed and rather slender. Collared lizards, as a group, are more brightly colored than the leopard lizards (see pages 94–95 for more description). These lizards are capable of bipedal locomotion.

Keeping: When housing collared and leopard lizards, you must always remember that all members of this group are both cannibalistic and highly predacious. Sexually mature male collared and leopard lizards are very territorial. Only a single adult male should be present in any enclosure. A hungry crotaphytine will eat smaller lizards, including such unpalatable-appearing types as spiny and horned lizards. Insects such as grasshoppers, crickets, beetles, and their larvae, are eagerly accepted.

Stressed lizards (such as newly captured specimens or those kept in less than ideal conditions) are more apt to suffer adversely from parasite infestations. An emaciated or dehydrated appearance often accompanies parasite overloads.

Crotaphytines will learn to drink from a water dish. Until acclimated,

Although most are wild caught, the desert collared lizard, Crotaphytus bicinctores, *is increasingly common in the pet trade.*

they may prefer lapping up droplets of water sprinkled on the stones in their enclosures.

Crotaphytine lizards will thrive as captives if healthy when received, if immediately purged of endoparasites, and if offered proper quarters and diet. Low relative humidity and a spacious cage with a substrate of several inches of dry sand are necessary. Rocks will be both appreciated and used extensively as a vantage point, especially if a heat lamp is directed at the highest point of the rocks.

We suggest a minimum floor space of 18 inches × 48 inches (45.7 cm × 122 cm) for a single specimen or a pair of these lizards, with more space being provided for more lizards.

A hotspot (up to 115°F, 46°C) for basking, a cooler resting area, and full-spectrum lighting are imperative. Night temperatures may drop

93

The eastern collared lizard, Crotaphytus collaris, *is now bred by many hobbyists. It is the most variable collared lizard species in coloration.*

necessary to trigger the physiological changes that culminate in successful reproductive activity. All crotaphytines are oviparous. From a few to as many as a dozen eggs are produced annually. Although dependent on temperature, incubation durations may vary from 55 to 90 days. It seems that an unnaturally high percentage of the eggs produced by captive crotaphytines kept in indoor terraria fail to develop. No one seems sure why this is so. Incubation in low-humidity conditions seems to most reliably result in hatchlings. Hatchlings are from 2.75 inches to 3.5 inches (7 cm–8.9 cm) in overall length.

Collared Lizards

Description: Look for collared lizards in boulder fields or on boulders along roadways. They often silhouette themselves by sitting on the tallest boulder where the view is unobscured. When frightened they run agilely downward from their vantage point into a burrow beneath it or an abutting boulder.

The collared lizards derive their name from the black collars that encircle the necks of most. These are better defined on males than on females. On some species, such as the protected reticulated collared lizard, *Crotaphytus reticulatus*, of south Texas, the collars are reduced to black spots.

Many males of the eastern collared lizard, *C. collaris*, are brightly colored. This is especially so during the hot days of late spring and of

into the 60s°F (18°C) with no ill effects to the lizards.

No more than a single male should be kept to a cage, but if rather similarly sized, a male and up to several females will usually cohabit well.

Breeding: Most crotaphytines hibernate to a greater or lesser degree. The duration of dormancy is considerably less in the South or in warmer lowlands than in the more northerly areas or at cooler, higher elevations. It is probable that a lengthy period of dormancy is

summer when the lizards are actively foraging and breeding. Males from more westerly areas of the range are often more brilliantly clad in blues, turquoise, and greens than those from more easterly populations. These latter bear more subdued tans, mauves, greens, and yellows. Eastern populations often have a tan head while in the west the head may be brilliant golden-yellow. Female eastern collared lizards tend to show less geographic variation, being tan to gray with brilliant orange highlights when gravid.

Whatever the geographic location, breeding and dominant male collared lizards are always the brightest.

The desert collared lizard, *C. bicinctores,* is a familiar sight through much of the far west. The body is tan and the mouth lining is light.

Since, once they feel cornered, collared lizards as a group are essentially fearless, and will leap up to a foot (30.5 cm) off the ground to firmly bite their aggressor, checking the color of the mouth lining is not as hard as it sounds. Merely peer inside while the lizard is firmly attached to your finger.

Leopard Lizards

The three species of the leopard lizards are clad in shades of brown and patterned with darker bars and spots. Breeding females are variously patterned with orange lateral markings.

Gambelia wislizenii, the long-nosed leopard lizard, may bear

Bearing conspicuous orange spots, gravid female long-nosed leopard lizards, Gambelia w. wislizenii, *are more colorful than breeding males.*

either a few large or a multitude of small dark dorsal and lateral spots. The short-nosed (*G. sila*) has no subspecies, but because habitat alteration due to agriculture and land development have diminished virtually all populations of this lizard, it is now a federally endangered species.

Chuckwallas and Desert Iguanas

Chuckwallas

Description: Chuckwallas are members of the once-again all-inclusive family, the Iguanidae.

The name chuckwalla came from the Cohuila Indian name of caxwal through the Spanish interpretation, chacahuala, to the present-day chuckwalla. These are heat-loving, fat-bellied, waddling lizards that dwell in rocky areas. Most are very wary even of approaching cars and crawl between rocks, inflate their bodies, and brace themselves with their legs when threatened. The thick tail will autotomize in either sex. Males are

The endangered piebald chuckwalla, Sauromalus varius, *of Mexico's San Esteban Island (Baja) is one of the largest of the chuckwallas and is only occasionally available to hobbyists.*

to San Esteban Island, and the spiny chuckwalla, *Sauromalus hispidus,* occurs on several Baja Islands, including Angel Island.

Across its range the common chuckwalla varies widely in color. From central Arizona southward to northern Sonora, Mexico, males are rather prominently tricolored. The head, shoulder, and forelimbs are black, the torso is brick red, the rear limbs are dark (the hind feet can be light), and the tail is cream, lightest dorsally. Near Phoenix, Arizona, male common chuckwallas are entirely jet black except for the tail, which is a brilliant fire-orange.

The chuckwallas of northern and western Arizona, southwestern Utah (including those of the Glen Canyon drainage), southern Nevada, southeastern California, and northern Baja are quite variable but compared to those of southern Arizona appear bleached. The adult males may have a pale red to yellow dorsum that may be moderately infiltrated with dark pigment. The tail may be yellow to red. Juveniles and females of the Glen Canyon drainage may be strongly banded in brick red. Males in Sonora tend to be a bit smaller than those further north.

The San Esteban chuckwalla has only recently (2006) become available to the casual hobbyist. It has a straw-tan ground color overlain with patches of darker pigment. The appearance gives rise to its other common name, the piebald chuckwalla. Usually the light pigment prevails over the dark pigment.

territorial and will select and defend a home range of about 30 square meters. Each range must have many projecting rocks around the range perimeter to serve as vantage points. Males engage in a ritualized series of head and body bobs when an interloping male approaches, and may actually leap off a perch to grab and tussle with an interloper that fails to heed the warning.

Of the three species of chuckwallas, only the common chuckwalla, *Sauromalus ater*, of the southwestern United States and northwestern Mexico is regularly seen in the pet trade. The remaining two species are larger than the common chuckwalla and are restricted to islands near the Baja California coast in the Sea of Cortez. These, the very large, endangered *Sauromalus varius*, the San Esteban chuckwalla, is endemic

The other insular species, the spiny chuckwalla, is large, heavy-bodied, and almost entirely black in color. The head and nape scales of the rough-necked chuckwalla are enlarged and tuberculate.

Keeping: Adult male chuckwallas are usually larger and are often more brightly colored than the females. The males are territorial, selecting a range with projecting rocks that serve as lookout points. In the spring, as breeding season begins, the males' femoral pores enlarge and are filled with a gray waxy substance that drags against the rocks as the male patrols his territory, leaving a distinctive chemical footprint for interloping males and unclaimed females. Those in captivity must be given desert-type caging with a single male per enclosure. They need a hot basking spot, elevated perching areas of rocks, and hiding areas large enough for the lizard(s) to withdraw entirely into.

Males will descend from their display area to feed. In very large enclosures housing multiple males, you may see the males feeding together but they will return to their perches and their defensive attitudes after feeding. The subdominate male(s) will feed after the dominant male feeds, but such a caging situation is a stressful one, not conducive to the health of any of the inhabitants.

Dominant males tend to sleep by themselves, but other chuckwallas may pile atop or against each other in a crevice. Chuckwallas may also elect to sleep atop a small flat perch, legs dangling over each side.

For diet, offer chuckwallas the same veggie diet as the green iguana, with a few insects such as mealworms or crickets added on an occasional basis. Chucks in the wild are vegetarian because chasing down and catching insects takes more energy than worthwhile. Instead, the lizards dine on flowers, leaves, and seeds of many desert plants. The range of the common chuckwalla roughly coincides with the range of the creosote bush, the leaves and blossoms of which form their major food source.

Chuckwallas engage in grooming behavior when they are actively shedding. The chuckwalla wishing to be groomed approaches another and crouches down in a subservient position. The second chuck bites off and consumes the skin. Either can end the session by moving away. Unlike geckos, chuckwallas are not known to consume their own skin.

Chuckwallas have a relatively short annual activity period. As would be expected from a large lizard in a temperate climate, they emerge from hibernation late in the year (mid- to late April, depending on the temperature) and retire again well before the cold weather has truly set in. While "up and about," chucks are active only during the warmest part of the day. A body temperature of 99 to 102°F (37–38.9°C) seems to be their operating optimum. At that temperature, they are active, alert, wary, and, for a big, heavy lizard, even somewhat agile.

The subtly colored but pretty little desert iguana,
Dipsosaurus dorsalis, *is a common lizard of our*
Southwest, of northwestern mainland Mexico,
and of northeastern Baja.

Breeding: Chuckwallas are oviparous lizards, the females digging a burrow and laying a single clutch consisting of from a few to nearly a dozen large eggs in mid- to late summer. It is conjectured that females in the wild produce their clutches only every other year. Captive females, traditionally better fed and having a somewhat longer annual activity period, may reproduce annually. Babies hatch in 60–90 days, depending on temperature and soil humidity.

These are ideal species for advanced hobbyists and zoological institutions.

The Desert Iguana or "Dipso"

It is from its generic name of *Dipsosaurus dorsalis* that the vernacular "dipso" comes for this little lizard. It is also known as the "desert iguana."

Description: Like that of the chuckwalla, the range of the desert iguana follows that of its major food plant, the creosote bush, and can be seen climbing into the branches of the creosote to feed on the leaves. Unlike the chuckwalla, which is a rock climber, the dipso prefers sand hummocks with patches of firm ground or clay surfaces and with some sheltering plants and scattered rocks. It digs burrows for refuge.

The desert iguana is an attractive lizard that likes to dart around its large cage. While heavy-bodied, it is not obese. It has a short head with a rounded snout, stout limbs, and a tapering tail that is about equal in length to that of the head and body. Except for the low vertebral crest, the body scales are small while those of the tail are large and arranged in prominent whorls.

While the ground color of *Dipsosaurus* varies somewhat (approximating the color of the sand in any given area), it always gives the appearance of a foot-long (30.5 cm) tan lizard. The ground color is sandy gray and overlain on the sides with a blush of brown or brownish red. Light ocelli are present anteriorly, wavy lines posteriorly.

Keeping: Given a desert-type terrarium with a hot spot and firm enough substrate to permit burrowing, rocks, and a herbivorous diet of mixed greens (avoid those containing oxalic acid), shredded carrots, dandelion leaves and blossoms, flowers, and buds, captive desert iguanas will thrive up to 15 years or more. Make sure the enclosure is brightly lit, with UV-enhanced lights.

Breeding: Desert iguanas will fare best if there is only a single male to the cage. Females can be kept together or with a single male. Males will begin to display to the females in early spring, with breeding taking place from April through July. The females dig burrows and deposit their three to eight eggs in mid- to late summer. Eggs hatch in later summer to early fall.

Spiny-tailed Agamids

The various species of the agamid lizard genus *Uromastyx* are variously known as spiny-tails, dabb lizards, and, most recently, by the diminutive of "uro." They may be considered the Old World counterpart of the desert iguana. Pudgy, unafraid lizards, some specimens adapt to captivity; most do not.

Description: There are between 13 and 17 species of *Uromastyx,* ranging in size from comparatively slender 14 inches (35.6 cm) (the Indian and Pakistani Indian spiny-tail, *U. hardwicki*) to a robust 36 inches plus (91 cm plus) (the Egyptian spiny tail, *U. aegyptius*). Hardwicki has so far proven to be the easiest to maintain in captivity. The ground color and intensity of pattern of spiny-tailed agamids is altered by temperature. When cool, the lizards are the dullest and darkest, the better to absorb the warmth of the sun. As the lizards warm, their colors lighten. The females of some species are both smaller and less colorful than the males.

Keeping: Uros need a desert terrarium, with a high-illumination level and UV-B availability, along with a sandy/clay substrate deep enough for burrowing.

The spiny-tailed lizards are inveterate tunnelers, at times constructing home burrows of 10 feet (3.05 m) or more in length. The burrows are often begun amidst rocks or near the root mass of a low shrub. When the lizards are "at home," they often plug the burrow with loose earth to help prevent moisture loss inside the burrow.

In the wild, the majority of the water required by these lizards is acquired from the vegetation they consume. Water needs are also met when body fat reserves are metabolized during "lean times." Captive

Breeding males of the ornate spiny-tailed agamid, Uromastyx o. ornatus, *are very brightly colored. This species is eagerly sought by hobbyists.*

Because of similar coloration the juveniles of many spiny-tailed lizards are difficult to differentiate to species. This is a juvenile North African Uromastyx acanthinurus.

uros will drink from a flat dish. It may be necessary to limit water access to control humidity. Care should be taken that the substrate does not become wet if the lizards walk through their water supply. In fact, to help preclude the possibility of respiratory ailments (often associated with abnormally high humidity and lower than optimum temperatures), always take all reasonable precautions to assure a low cage humidity for all species of spiny-tails.

The preferred diet of wild uros is tough and nonsucculent leaves and blossoms of *Artemesia* and related composites (wormwood, cudweed, tarragon). Captive spiny-tailed agamids should be provided with a basic herbivorous lizard diet to which is added fresh and dried peas, pelleted alfalfa, fresh beans of all types, wild bird seed, and millet. Other seeds may also be consumed. Slightly moistened chick starter mash, available in most farm feed stores, is a good dietary supplement. The standard vegetables offered should consist of kale, various greens (no spinach or chard), grated vegetables, some fruit, and suitable blossoms when available. The blossoms and leaves of the common dandelion, hibiscus, and nasturtium are relished and are highly nutritious.

Although most spiny-tails show great interest in, and will readily consume crickets and other insects, avoid insect foods because of potential health problems.

Uros may be sexed by color intensity for some species, and the femoral pores of the males tend to be larger than those of the females. When kept communally, keep one male to each group. The females will form their own hierarchies and you'll need to watch the group to ensure that all are feeding and have an opportunity to thermoregulate under the hotspot. Even low levels of aggression will rather quickly debilitate subordinate specimens.

Breeding: All members of the genus are oviparous. Of the numerous species, only five are seen with

MIL

3534

5/11/2018
Pickup By:

PUBLIC

2198202254612Z

Lizard care from A to Z

Lizard care from A to Z

21982022576122

PUBLIC

Pickup By:
5/11/2018

3534

MIL

any regularity in the American and European pet trades.

U. hardwicki, the Indian spiny-tail, is common on certain sections of the hard-pan plains of India and Pakistan. They are not a colorful species but they do seem adaptable. Clad in scales of olive gray, dull olive green, or charcoal, cold specimens are especially dark. When at ideal body temperatures a varying degree of olive-yellow pigment is present. *U. hardwicki* was once exported by Pakistani collectors to both Europe and America in rather large numbers. This species seems more able than many other *Uromastyx* to adapt to the high humidities normally present in the southeastern United States. If provided with suitably high temperatures (88 to 105°F [31–41°C]) and a diet that is suitably high in vegetation and seeds, some *U. hardwicki* will thrive. This is no longer a commonly seen species in the pet trade, but occasional specimens are still available. Our specimens were personable and unafraid and took dandelion leaves and blossoms from our fingers.

U. aegyptius is rather like a gigantic Indian spiny-tail in appearance. It, too, thrives on hot temperatures, dryness and a 95 percent vegetable/seed diet. This is the largest of the spiny-tails, with occasional specimens nearing a yard (91 cm) in total length. Egyptian spiny-tails were common in both American and European pet trades in the early 1990s, but a tightening of the export laws may soon render these impressively large lizards virtually unavailable.

One of the most variably and beautifully colored of the spiny-tailed lizards is the North African *U. acanthinurus.* It is also one of the hardiest. Darkest on the head and the tail, when this species is suitably warm, much of its body is suffused with tans, reds, yellows, and greens. A moderately sized species, *U. acanthinurus,* attains a length of about 15 inches (38 cm). These pretty lizards are now being bred in the American Southwest. They are long-lived animals; a pair kept indoors in Miami survived for more than 20 years.

A very few of the Arabian *U. benti* are occasionally imported to America. This is another moderately sized species with a sandy ground color and prominent dorsal barring.

Two races of the very attractive *U. ocellatus* are rather regularly imported to both America and Europe at present. These are *U. o. ocellatus,* the ocellated, and *U. o. ornatus,* the ornate, spiny tails. The females of both are of a sandy hue, often with dorsal and lateral barring and ocellations. The males of both are colorful, but healthy, optimally warmed males of the aptly named ornate spiny-tail are spectacularly so. These are suffused with intensely bright turquoises and russets and are among the world's most beautifully colored lizards. This lizard is

Like true geckos, the night lizards are devoid of functional eyelids. They are small, often spotted, denizens of the arid lands. This is a Bezy's night lizard, Xantusia bezyi.

Description: Night lizards are slightly depressed in general conformation. They have no eyelids. The eyes are protected by a clear scale (the brille) and the pupils are vertically elliptical. Belly scales are much larger than the dorsal scales, and a raised line or ridge of skin delineates the lateral from the belly scales. The tail is very easily autotomized. Males have enlarged femoral pores and a wider tail base than females.

These primarily nocturnal lizards are very secretive. They rest behind exfoliating rock slabs, in bark crevices, and beneath vegetation by day, emerging with darkness to look for insects. They seek cover at the slightest disturbance.

Species within the genus *Lepidophyma* are loosely called the greater night lizards. Temperate species are found largely amid desert plants (yuccas) and on exfoliating rock outcroppings. Tropical species inhabit both savannas and forested areas and are often found behind shards of loosened bark on still-standing trees. About 15 species are in the group. Lepidophymas are small lizards, the biggest being about five inches (13 cm) long. They are very quietly colored in shades of tan to brown with olive overtones. They are robust little lizards, with the tail about the same length as the body. Males have larger heads and larger femoral pores than the females. *L. smithi* and *L. flavimaculatus* are widely distributed in Latin America and are the only two members of the genus seen in the pet trade.

currently present in fairly large numbers in several captive breeding facilities in the southwestern United States and in smaller numbers in indoor facilities in Europe.

Night Lizards

The Xantusiidae is a small family of four genera, which in turn are split up (depending on the authority) into a dozen to a dozen and a half species. These nondescript, big-eyed lizards are not well known in the pet trade, although a few species of *Lepidophyma* are occasionally offered by dealers. All are small—to perhaps six inches (15 cm)—live-bearers from southwestern American, Mexican, and Central American regions. Several of the species are associated with exfoliating desert rocks.

Tropical night lizards (this is Lepidophyma flavimaculatus) *are quite arboreal. They may be found behind bark shards and in similar habitats on savannas and in scrub forests of Mexico and Central America.*

The other night lizard genus of the pet trade is *Xantusia.* Only one, the desert night lizard (*X. vigilis*) is offered to hobbyists with any regularity. This five-inch-long (13 cm) (usually smaller) species is brown, and may have darker spots on its dorsum. Males have larger femoral pores that give the thigh a more angular appearance in cross-section than the female's. The preferred habitat of some populations seems to be inside of, or beneath, decomposing yucca plants or Joshua trees. In other areas it is a lizard of rock exfoliations.

Another species, *X. henshawi,* the granite night lizard, is prettily marked. Its color and pattern assures that it will blend well with the mineral for which it is named. It occurs in southwestern California and adjacent Baja, and is sometimes seen scuttling up the exterior walls of houses, much like a house gecko. It is small, about five inches (13 cm), and is capable of considerable color changes. Often it sports gray spots on light (almost white) dorsum. Males display a light oval patch along the leading edge of the femoral pores.

Keeping: In captivity, night lizards need desert terraria. If the nighttime temperatures are allowed to drop, some specimens may use a hotspot for morning thermoregulation before going into seclusion for the day; however, most prefer to bask beneath a warmed rock or bark slab. Captive night lizards will feed on small crickets, mealworms, beetles, grasshoppers, and other "bite-sized" insects.

Breeding: Night lizards are livebearers. Depending on the species, they will have one to seven tiny babies in late summer or early autumn. Tropical species may breed year round.

Skinks

Desert Skinks

Many of the world's skinks are desert and/or arid savanna dwellers. Of these, comparatively few appear in the pet trades of America and Europe. All of the few species we discuss here are primarily insectivorous, but most will lap at a fruit-honey mixture (see page 164 for formula) or eat an occasional piece of sweet fruit.

Description: Most skink species are difficult to sex. Fully adult males may be larger, stockier, and more brilliantly colored than fully adult females. The differences in coloration are most pronounced when males are in breeding readiness. During this period the heads of the males of some species may develop bilateral temporal "swellings."

Keeping: Because of their rather small size and secretive habits, these skinks can all be maintained in fairly small terraria. We suggest a minimum floor space of 12 inches x 30 inches (30.5 cm × 76 cm) (the size of a 20-gallon-long [75.7 L] aquarium) for a single specimen or a pair. We use larger tanks (up to 18 inches × 48 inches [45.7 cm × 122 cm] floor dimensions; 75-gallon volume [284 L]) for breeding groups. As with most lizards, multiple males may be antagonistic, especially during the breeding season. Females are more tolerant of others of their sex. We suggest that breeding groups be limited to a single male and from one to five females. Strive for a similarity in size. Smaller lizards may be injured by larger ones; baby lizards may be eaten by adults. As with any lizards, check frequently (especially during the breeding season) to ascertain that the lizards within the group remain compatible. Remove specimens that are persecuted by their cagemates.

Breeding: Little is known about the captive breeding of any of these desert skinks and there seems to be no foolproof method of inducing reproduction. We have found that only well-fed females ovulate, often only if having undergone a period of winter cooling and winter reduction of photoperiod. We have bred Great Plains skinks some years after fully hibernating them for a 60- to 90-day period. On other years identical cycling procedures have not induced breeding.

Ocellated or Barrel Skinks

The ocellated skinks are not as popular with American hobbyists as with our European counterparts. Perhaps the best-known species is the subtly but prettily colored ocellated skink, *Chalcides ocellatus.* Wild-collected specimens of the ocellated skink are currently readily available in the pet trades of the world. The ocellations from which *C. ocellatus* takes both its common and specific names are rather regularly arranged on both the back and sides of this little lizard.

Chalcides ocellatus, *the ocellated skink, is a persistent burrower in aridland habitats of southern Europe and northern Africa.*

Description: *C. ocellatus* varies widely in size. While some of these skinks barely exceed a six-inch (15 cm) overall length when adult, others may near, or attain, a full foot (30.5 cm) in length. The legs of the ocellated skink are short but fully functional. This species has colonized variable habitats and may be found in seaside wrack or in high and dry olive groves, vineyards, or sparsely wooded natural savannas. It prefers dry areas and may be very common on rocky plains and semi-deserts. The ocellated skink is agile and alert, diving quickly beneath ground cover when startled. It is also quite adept at sandswimming.

Keeping: This hardy species will thrive in both desert or dry savanna set-ups. To attain proper sand-moisture, see the comments we have made regarding the sandfish on page 108.

Breeding: *C. ocellatus* is viviparous. Clutches may number from four to more than ten babies. It is a widely distributed species, ranging from southern Europe to northern Africa and southwest Asia. Males of this difficult-to-sex skink are larger and somewhat heavier than females.

Remember that specimens from the more northerly part of the range will require somewhat lower temperatures and fewer hours of daylight during reproductive cycling than those from the South. Many European hobbyists fully hibernate ocellated skinks of European origin.

To lessen the draw on wild populations, we should do everything possible to promote the captive propagation of this hardy lizard.

Jet black with a deep blue tail and white facial spots when a hatchling, the Great Plains skink, Plestiodon obsoletus, *is olive-tan flecked with profuse darker markings when adult.*

Great Plains Skink

Description: Unlike its eastern relatives, the wide-ranging Great Plains skink, *Plestiodon obsoleta,* is not striped. It occurs in our central and western states and adjacent Mexico. Hatchlings are jet black except for white dots on the sides of the face and a royal blue tail. The adults vary from fawn to tan in ground color and are heavily reticulated with black on the back and sides. Adults have a yellowish venter. This may well be the largest skink to occur in America. The record size is

a hefty 13.75 inches (34.9 cm). Some reproductively active male Great Plains skinks may develop a vague orange flush on the widened head, but, many do not. Generally speaking, this skink is difficult to sex.

Keeping: See general discussion of keeping skinks, page 104.

Breeding: For our Great Plains skinks to cycle reproductively, it has been necessary for us to hibernate them for between two and three months. They are oviparous. The food insects or prepared foods of gestating females should be enhanced with calcium-D_3 additives twice or three times weekly. Fast-growing hatchlings may require the calcium-D_3 supplements daily. Large females may produce 20 or more eggs, but 8 to 12 is a more usual clutch size. Eggs produced by our females have hatched in from 50 to 60 days at a temperature of 80 to 86°F (26.7–30°C).

Schneider's and Algerian Skinks

Specimens of the nominate race of the Schneider's skink, *Novoeumeces s. schneideri* are still readily available in both American and European pet trades.

Description: The ground color of this foot long (30.5 cm) lizard varies from buff to pearl gray. The dorsum is spotted or vaguely barred with orange. These are beautiful, aggressive, and seldom bred Asian and North African lizards.

Although it was once a commonly seen pet trade species, the big *N. algeriensis,* a North African species of rocky semideserts and savannas, is now a comparative rarity. It is much more placid than the rest of the group. Rather than orange spots, *N. algeriensis* has orange crossbars that are bordered anteriorly by black-edged, white ocelli. It is one of the larger species in the complex, attaining a heavy-bodied foot to 14 inches (30.5–35.6 cm) in total length.

Males of the *schneideri*-complex skinks are larger and somewhat more colorful than females, and may develop heavy jowls, especially during the breeding season.

Both the Schneider's skink, Novoeumeces s. schneideri *(top), and the Algerian skink,* N. algeriensis, *make hardy pets that become quite tame.*

Nevertheless, the sexes can be difficult to differentiate.

Keeping: Most of these skinks are cold tolerant, hence ideal for hobbyists in temperate climes. Besides the normal diet of insects, many of these skinks will readily accept prepared foods and some fruit. They will thrive in either desert or savanna terraria. We have also kept them outside in the large metal rings (page 19). Like most aridland

The large and very unusual-appearing giant sandfish, Scincus festatus, *(top), is less often seen in the pet trade than the more colorful common sandfish* S. scincus *(bottom).*

perature varies from about 80°F (26.7°C) (cool end) to a sand-surface temperature of 100 to 105°F (37.8–40.6°C) beneath the basking light.

Breeding: The *schneideri*-complex skinks are all oviparous. Few breeding successes have been reported with these skinks and much work on their reproductive cycles remains to be done. Average clutch sizes are unknown. The pet trade remains entirely dependent on wild-collected specimens, a situation we consider untenable.

Sandfish

There are about ten species in the genus *Scincus.* All are desert-dwelling skinks commonly known as sandfish. The task of attaining taxonomic stability is rendered difficult by a paucity of knowledge and the fact that many of the species are ontogenetically and geographically variable.

Description: Members of this genus may be encountered in arid-land, loose sand habitats, from eastern northern Africa to Pakistan. Despite the fact that they are accomplished burrowers, there is no trend toward reduction in limb size; however, the toes are flattened with serrate flanges on the trailing edges.

These lizards are all so similar in general appearance that once their exact origin has been lost in the pet trade traffic, they are difficult to identify with certainty. The eyelids are well developed and functional and the lower jaw is noticeably countersunk, a feature that pre-

and savanna lizards, these skinks thermoregulate extensively. Those kept outside would bask on rocks having a surface temperature of more than 100°F (37.8°C). We provide them daytime thermal gradients in indoor terraria. During the summer, the nighttime temperature is about 70°F (21°C). The daytime tem-

vents the loose sand from entering the lizard's mouth.

It is probable that most sandfish being imported at the moment by the pet trades of both America and Europe are *S. s. scincus,* the common sandfish; however, at least a few specimens of the eastern sandfish, *S. mitranus* have recently become available. Of the two, it is the eastern that is the more colorful, having a ground color of yellow to yellow-ochre (males) to tan (subadults). Both sexes have a series of broad dorsal crossbands, but, again, these are best defined on male specimens. The pale-colored subspecies, *S. s. conirostris,* is remarkably similar in external features to *S. mitranus.* Females are the smaller sex.

Keeping: *Scincus* should be provided with as large a terrarium as possible. Ours are maintained with up to a foot (30.5 cm) of fine sand. Keep in mind how heavy this is when designing a stand for the terrarium. The bottom layer of sand is kept barely moistened by trickling a little water down a vertical PVC standpipe that reaches from above the level of the sand to the glass aquarium bottom. The water is drawn away from the standpipe by capillary action.

Although they are probably more apt to seek their prey while walking on top of the sand, sandfish may approach it submarine fashion from below. They eagerly consume small beetles (particularly favoring small June beetles), tenebrionid beetles and their larvae, spiders, and other suitably sized arthropods. When conditions are favorable, sandfish can derive most of their moisture needs from the moist bottom layers of terrarium sand and from their insect prey; however, when their terrarium is too dry, sandfish will drink from a low receptacle. The suggested sand-surface daytime temperature at the hot end of their tank is about 110°F (43°C). The cool end of the tank can be 85°F (29°C). Nighttime temperatures of both the hot and cool end of the terrarium can be allowed to drop by another several degrees.

Breeding: At present, despite the fact that they are apt to be secretive, sandfish are immensely popular in the pet marketplace. Captive lifespans in excess of ten years have been documented. Although these skinks are often reported to bear live young they are actually oviparous. About six eggs are laid in each clutch. Two females held by us produced small clutches (two and four) of inviable soft-shelled eggs. In one case, while cleaning a terrarium, we found four babies beneath a deeply buried rock. Since the lower levels of the terrarium sand was infrequently disturbed, the eggs from which these emerged were not seen, nor were remnants of eggshells found.

Chapter Ten
The Savanna Terrarium

Savannas are areas of transition between or at the edge of forests, woodlands, or deserts. Spacious, rolling glades, these often sparsely vegetated areas are home to a great many lizard species. Different soil composition and formation and a variable but moderated rainfall provide a habitat much different from that of either surrounding desert or woodland/forest. Savannas often host various species of moderately, or at least seasonally, lush grasses, as well as thornscrub and other formidably armed trees. Areas of rocky scree may be present.

Savannas are often subjected to weather extremes in the form of temperature, rainfall, or other such climatic vagaries. The plant community found in savannas is difficult to maintain in terraria over extended periods. Periodic refurbishing of your terrarium vegetation will most likely be necessary.

A thick layer of sandy humus into which a liberal helping of variably sized rocks have been mixed should comprise the substrate of the savanna terrarium. Seedling acacias and clumped grasses, as well as weathered branches, cactus skeletons, and strategically placed rocks

and rock formations can be used for decorative purposes. The savanna terrarium plant community will require somewhat more water than those in the desert terrarium; however, even with judicious care, many (especially the grasses) will need replacing each season. The plants can be either potted or planted directly into the terrarium substrate. We prefer the latter, for many savanna lizard species enjoy digging their burrows into and beneath the plant's root systems. A screen top will be helpful in keeping the low humidity preferred by most savanna-dwelling lizards.

Since we will be discussing many very diverse lizard species in the following pages, we will not generalize on the size and husbandry needed.

Geckos

Keeping: Providing additional vitamins and minerals for captive geckos is an important consideration. To this end, for the insect eaters, dust the crickets with a finely powdered supplement that contains both calcium and vitamin D_3. These supplements need to be provided at least once a week (twice weekly when quickly growing baby geckos are present). If your geckos are nectar feeders, provide a vitamin-enhanced fruit concoction like that suggested in the *Phelsuma* description (see page 164).

Although most of the terrestrial geckos can and will drink from a water dish, the arboreal geckos need to be misted daily. Be sure that at least some of the plants in the tanks retain pendulous droplets for the geckos to drink.

Breeding: Inducing breeding may involve nothing more complex than placing both sexes together, or it can be a little more complicated. Ovulation and spermatogenesis may be controlled by photoperiod (day length), relative humidity, and temperature. Thus, we have found almost all gecko species breed seasonally, beginning with the lengthening days of spring and progressing into egg laying with the heightened relative humidity in late spring and with the early summer rains. Mimicking these phenomena is rather easily done within the confines of a terrarium. By increasing the hours of illumination, misting the tank a little more frequently, and making subtle temperature alterations, you may be able to induce breeding by your geckos.

Those geckos that you intend to breed should be stocky (not obese) and endoparasite free. Thin geckos will produce fewer eggs and more delicate embryos. An egg-deposition area suitable to the needs of the species with which you are working

must be provided. In the case of arboreal species, this may be vertical pieces of bamboo or sturdy plants such as *Sanseveria*. For terrestrial species a low (two-inch [5.1 cm]) margarine cup containing barely moistened sand or vermiculite may be nestled into the sand near one corner. When properly set up, the females will seldom fail to use the deposition site. If possible, the eggs should be removed on the morning following deposition and placed in a temperature-controlled styrofoam incubator. Eggs attached to the glass will be impossible to remove. Tape a small plastic cup containing a little barely dampened sphagnum (the moss should not touch the eggs) over the eggs.

Territoriality (male-to-male sparring and territory protection) may be employed to induce breeding. After successfully backing down an opponent, a dominant male gecko will often dash to a female, indulge in courtship, and breed her.

Although some of the little sphaerodactyline geckos might be termed egg scatterers (merely laying their hard-shelled eggs amid the leaf litter of the woodland floor), other sphaerodactylines seek out specific sites and may place their eggs in treetrunk hollows or in bark crevices, sometimes several feet above the ground. The rather thick-shelled eggs of the sphaerodactylines resist both desiccation and over-hydration.

Other female geckos, among them some of the house geckos,

Helmeted geckos, Geckonia chazaliae, *do well if kept in small groups. They communicate by making soft clicking sounds.*

may also merely place their eggs among the leaves, but these geckos seem to choose an area. Frequently their chosen deposition sites are also protected by additional debris or litter. Hollows beneath rocks, cinder blocks, logs, boards, newspapers, or discarded roofing shingles are seemingly favored.

The eggs of some gecko species have adhesive shells and are placed high in hollow trees or near the eaves in buildings where they remain until hatching. One such gecko is the tokay. The paired eggs are laid in an area chosen by the female. As she places the eggs with her hind feet, their shells are drying, and by the time she has accomplished her task, the eggs have adhered and will remain for the duration. So effective is the adhesion of the eggs that pieces of the hatched shells often remain in place for years, providing evidence of multiple clutching and even communal nesting practices.

With more than 700 species known, of which more than 50 are frequently seen in the pet trade, it was difficult to choose a few representative species to discuss here. At least some members of the four general types listed below are true pet trade favorites.

Helmeted Gecko

The single species of this genus is the interesting, terrestrial, *Geckonia chazaliae.*

Description: This is a fairly small but big-headed and robust gecko. As an adult it is about 3.5 inches (8.8 cm) in overall length, of which half is tail.

This is an aridland species from North Africa. It seems to prefer rocky and gravelly areas.

Weather permitting, *Geckonia* is active year round. It is capable of brumating for short periods if necessary. Both crepuscular and nocturnal in nature, captives may also forage by day, especially when in reduced light situations.

The helmeted gecko can produce low clicking notes.

This desert and dry savanna gecko is clad in earthen-colored scales. The background color can vary from reddish buff to pale gray. Dark and/or light markings may or may not be present. The tuberculate scales are irregular in size. The enlarged conical scales at the rear of the large head give this lizard its common name. The lidless eyes are heavily browed. The short, sturdy legs bear short and flattened toes with serrate scales along the edges. The toes are webbed at their bases.

Male helmeted geckos have a bulbous tail base.

Keeping: *Geckonia* is normally slow moving. When startled it is capable of quick movement but captives move in short bursts. Their small size allows them to thrive in a 15-gallon (56.8 L) capacity terrarium with a substrate of a couple of inches of sand and small rocks. When still, the little geckos are almost invisible against the terrarium substrate. This undemanding gecko species thrives in daytime temperatures of 85 to 96°F (29–35.6°C) and nighttime temperatures in the 70s°F (20s°C); heat tapes can be used to maintain the daytime warmth. A winter rest period is induced by allowing the temperature to drop an additional ten degrees for one month. Although helmeted geckos will drink readily from a low water dish, they seem to need little moisture. Ours preferred to eat mealworms and beetles, but after a few weeks would pursue and eat nearly any insects offered. We fed our helmeted geckos sparingly during their winter cooling.

Helmeted geckos are rather easy to keep, but may present occasional challenges. One, a pair, or even a trio, will do well in a rocky savanna terrarium with separate hiding areas for each. Because these geckos are small and rather inactive, we have occasionally kept them in terraria with a floor space of 10 inches × 20 inches (25 cm × 50 cm)—a ten-gallon (37.8 L) tank. However, because we prefer to provide a greater amount of space whenever possible, a trio of these geckos is more often housed in a terrarium of at least 20-gallon-long (75.7 L) (floor space of 12 inches × 30 inches [30.5 cm × 76 cm]) size.

Breeding: Helmeted geckos are being bred both in the United States and in Europe on a limited basis. At 86°F (30°C) the eggs hatch in about 70 days. Our only female delivered three clutches at about 23-day intervals. All eggs were fertile.

Tokay and Related Geckos

Description: The 25 plus members of this wide-ranging, mostly Asiatic genus *Gekko* are nocturnal, with vertically elliptical pupils. The tail is about equal in length to the SVL. The southeast Asian *G. gecko*, may be the second most frequently sold gecko in the world (surpassed in popularity only by the leopard gecko)—this despite the fact that it has one of the worst dispositions of any species. Tokays have formidably powerful jaws and do not usually hesitate to bite any object that offends them, including the hands of keepers.

The tokay gecko attains about a foot (30.5 cm) in length. Of Asiatic origin, the tokay gecko is now a familiar sight in the wild in some areas of southern peninsula Florida. Not only is it the largest of the established alien geckos of Florida, it is also the loudest. The sharp "geck-o, geck-o, geck-o-o-ooo" calls of the males of this rather firmly established species resound on warm spring and summer nights from areas of seclusion in many parts of southern Florida.

Although basically nocturnal, these big geckos may sun on mornings following cool nights. Tokays hunt and consume vertebrate and invertebrate prey, ranging from other lizards, frogs, insects and other arthropods, to nestling birds and rodents. When they perceive an enemy, tokays open their mouth, voice a drawn-out "Gecccck" and then bite. They may hang on, tightening up at intervals. This can be a distressing encounter for an unsuspecting person.

These are very predaceous lizards, with an unforgettable coloration of orange and white markings against a gray or blue-gray ground color. The bulging eyes are yellow-green to orange, and sink into the head when the tokay bites. The toepads are flattened and have clinging lamallae on the underside that enables this lizard to easily walk up virtually any vertical surface, including glass.

Male tokays are the larger and slightly more colorful sex. They have larger preanal pores than the females and a heavier tail base.

Breeding: Males are very vocal at breeding time. Breeding may occur during most months of the year in captivity, and may often be stimulated by lowered barometric pressure and misting. Truthfully, tokays do not require much preparation, other than good body weight, to induce breeding activities. Females lay hard-shelled, paired, adhesive-shelled eggs in elevated secluded areas, up to several times a year. The young exceed three inches (7.6 cm) at hatching. Communal nestings occur.

Because it is showy and inexpensive, the large and often defensive tokay gecko, Gekko gecko, is popular with hobbyists. Most are collected from the wild and will bite if handled or restrained.

The Indonesian Skunk Gecko

Description: Another member of this genus is the Indonesian skunk or white-striped gecko from Indonesia and Oceania. *Gekko vittatus* is a slender and attractive species that

Despite their name, not all skunk geckos, Gekko vittatus, *have a vertebral stripe.*

is fairly new to the pet trade. It commonly attains a length of more than eight inches (20 cm). The morph from which the popular name was derived is the most frequently seen. This morph displays a broad white vertebral stripe that forks on the nape. One prong extends anteriorly to the rear of each eye. The stripe often extends rearward onto the basal first fifth of the tail. Distal from that point the tail markings are in the form of rings.

Individuals in some populations of *G. vittatus* may lack the vertebral stripe entirely. These specimens often have irregular splotches of white or light pigment on the dorsal and lateral surfaces. The light markings may be most prominent on the limbs and tail. The skunk gecko does not seem as vocal as the tokay.

Keeping: Although they are often kept (and have even bred) in terraria as small as ten gallons (37.8 L) in volume, we feel that these large, active, territorial geckos should be provided much more space than this. Since they are highly arboreal,

we also suggest that a vertically oriented terrarium be used wherever possible. Our tokays, and related large species, are most often kept in our outside walk-in cages that have inside measurements of approximately 48 inches long × 30 inches wide × 66 inches high (122 cm × 76 cm × 168 cm). They do very well and breed readily in these wire-covered, wood-framed cages. We suggest a minimum terrarium size of 55 gallons (208 L) that can be stood on end to afford a vertical aspect.

Breeding: Males of the skunk gecko have a more bulbous tail base and larger preanal pores than females. Captives have produced eggs in nearly every month of the year, but seem most stimulated to breed during the lengthening days of spring. Egg deposition and incubation is the same for this species as for the tokay gecko.

Australian Velvet Geckos

Description: The 13 or so species in the Australian genus *Oedura* have well-developed (but variably

configured) distally divided toepads. In all cases the most distal pair of lamellae are the largest. The claws are retractile and the pupils vertically elliptical. The scalation is homogeneous. All are of nocturnal habits. The tails of all *Oedura* are easily autotomized; regenerated tails are often short and bulbous.

Most species contained within this genus are coveted by herpetoculturists worldwide. They are of moderate size, attenuate build, not particularly nervous, and quite hardy and easily cared for. All can be bred, and some of them rather easily and prolifically. Adding to the desirability is the fact that, in keeping with Australia's restrictive wildlife exportation policies, none, even of the more easily bred species, are yet abundant in herpetoculture, thus they hold their prices well.

The species of *Oedura* seen most commonly in both American and European herpetoculture is *Oedura castelnaui*, the northern velvet gecko. This pretty gecko attains an overall length of about six inches (15 cm).

The northern velvet gecko is restricted in distribution to the eastern slopes of northern New South Wales and southern Queensland, Australia. It is both arboreal in dry sclerophyll forest and saxicolous (rock dwelling). It shelters beneath loosened bark shards and in rocky crevices and exfoliations.

This is another tropical gecko species that is active virtually year round. Although basically nocturnal, northern velvet geckos are also crepuscular to a degree. Captives are occasionally active by day.

Typical gecko clicks and squeaks are produced by male northern velvet geckos.

The hatchlings and juveniles of the northern velvet gecko are more precisely marked than the adults. Young specimens are attractively clad in a chocolate-colored dorsum on which several broad, light gray or buff crescents or rounded chevrons are superimposed. The center of the light areas may contain a few russet or peach-colored scales. With growth and age the peach coloration becomes more profuse, breaking up or at least diffusing the dark dorsal areas. Of the three colors, it is the lightest that remains the most constant.

Albino specimens are known and are currently being propagated in captivity.

No tuberculate scales are present on dorsal or lateral surfaces.

Keeping: Although alert, this gecko is not overly active. A pair or trio will do well in a vertically oriented 15-gallon (56.8 L) tank (a 15-gallon "high" is also ideal). Of course, larger tanks can be used if preferred. Layered, vertically oriented corkbark pieces provide ideal hiding areas for these lovers of solitude and darkness. Stiff-leaved plants (sanseverias, etc.) provide hiding areas and visual barriers. A temperature of 80 to 90°F (26.7–32°C) is perfectly acceptable for these geckos. Males may be identified by the bulging hemipenial area at the tail base and their proportionately larger preanal pores. Small insects, spiders, and, occasionally, worms will be accepted by velvet geckos. They are hardy and ideal captives, suitable for either novice or advanced hobbyists.

Although they drink pendulous droplets of water from plants and perches, many will also learn to drink from a water dish that is placed close to their hiding areas. This is especially true if the surface of the water is roiled by an aquarium's air stone and/or is elevated somewhat.

Breeding: Members of this genus produce soft-shelled eggs that are buried in an easily worked, barely moistened, substrate. At a temperature of 84 to 87°F (28.9–30.6°C), incubation will last for about 60 days.

Some examples of the Sarasins' giant gecko, Rhacodactylus serasinorum*, bear an interesting light bridle. This 6-inch-long (15-cm) gecko and the very popular crested gecko are giants in name only.*

New Caledonian Geckos

Description: These geckos are just gaining in herpetocultural popularity. Of the genus *Rhacodactylus*, several smaller species are now regularly available in the pet trades of the United States and Europe. *Rhacodactylus auriculatus* seems, at the moment, to be the most commonly available species as well as the least expensive. While large in comparison to many species of geckos, this eight inch (20.3 cm) species is small when compared to others in the genus. It occurs in both a banded/mottled and a striped morph. Next most frequently seen is *R. serasinorum*. This sexually dimorphic species is rather prettily colored and slightly larger than the last. The remaining species of the genus are offered very infrequently and are usually prohibitively

117

With an adult size of 11 to 12 inches (28–30 cm), the heavy-bodied Rhacodactylus leachianus *truly is New Caledonia's giant gecko.*

expensive. One, *R. leachianus*, is the largest gecko species known in the world today. It attains a heavy-bodied, short-tailed, 14.5 inches (36.8 cm) in total length. Hatchlings command more than $1,000 each and adults sell for several times that amount. The somewhat smaller *R. trachyrhynchos* is one of the world's few live-bearing gecko species.

No species of *Rhacodactylus* could be considered brightly colored. Many are rich brown to gray when hatchlings/neonates and may either retain those colors or assume a dull greenish tinge when adult. All are capable of subtle individual color changes. No matter the base color, the profuse lichenate mottlings and shadings render them among the most wonderfully camouflaged of geckos. All are hardy, rather slow-moving species that, although initially slow to command the attention of herpetoculturists, are now coming into their own.

All eagerly accept both insects and various fruits as well as the fruit-honey mixture favored by the day geckos of the genus *Phelsuma* (see formula, page 164).

Keeping: The terrarium size should vary by the species and number to be maintained. We prefer 30-gallon (114 L) high (24 inches long × 12 inches wide × 24 inches high [61 cm × 30.5 cm × 61 cm]) terraria for the smaller species and 55-gallon (208 L) show tanks (48 inches long × 12 inches wide × 18 inches high [122 cm × 30.5 cm × 46 cm]) for the larger species.

The newest of the New Caledonian geckos to become available to the American pet trade is the eyelashed gecko, *R. ciliatus*. It is a five- or six-inch-long (13–15 cm) species that seems very hardy and easily bred. It is found hiding beneath ground debris during the day, but becomes at least partially arboreal while foraging at night. This species is now being captive bred in quite considerable numbers and may prove to be the easiest of the genus to breed.

Breeding: Males of all species in this genus have bulbous hemipenial bulges at the base of their tail. Little cycling, other than maintaining a natural photoperiod, seems necessary to induce breeding. A gentle evening misting with tepid water may induce activity and stimulate breeding. The rather soft-shelled eggs are not strongly adhesive and are laid in suitably concealed areas of the terrarium. Depending on the species and the individual, the eggs may be buried or merely laid on top of the substrate. Many of these geckos will preferentially enter a covered deposition box (with an entry hole cut in the top) containing moistened vermiculite or sphagnum. At a temperature in the low to mid-80s°F (27–29°C), incubation can take from two to three months, varying again by species and by substrate temperature.

Curly-tailed Lizards

Description: The genus *Leiocephalus* is large, consisting of about 20 plus species of robust West Indian lizards of moderate size. They are now in the family Tropiduridae (subfamily Leiocephalinae). Their common name, curly-tailed lizard, is derived from their resting pose; when startled or when coming to rest after a period of activity, many curl the distal two thirds (or more) of their tails upwards in a half (or even more complete) circle.

Although some of the smaller species are adult at about six

inches (15 cm) in total length, some larger species may exceed ten inches (25 cm). Tail length accounts for considerably more than half the total length.

Two, and possibly three, members of this tropical family are now colonized in southern Florida. The most successful of these is the long-established northern curly-tailed lizard, the Bahamian *Leiocephalus carinatus armouri*. It has been here the longest, seems to be expanding its range yearly, and is the dullest in color.

Curly-tails are clad in keeled scales of brown to tan, lighter laterally, and with obscure darker markings dorsally. A prominent, but low, vertebral crest is characteristic of lizards of this genus.

These lizards particularly favor rock piles or piles of concrete building rubble. Although primarily terrestrial, northern curly-tails are quick to take to the trees if pursued, and agile in avoiding capture.

Two red-sided curly-tailed lizards, *L. s. schreibersii* and *L. personatus scalaris*, have long been

Leiocephalus personatus scalaris is known as the green-legged curly-tailed lizard. This Hispaniolan native is now established in south Florida.

Although called a curly-tailed lizard, the red-sided Leiocephalus s. schreibersii *does not curl its tail tightly.*

secluded in below-ground retreats for periods of several days at a time. They also may remain secluded on overcast or rainy days even in the summer. The soft-shelled eggs number from two to ten and at 82 to 86°F (27.8–30°C) hatch in from 60 to 75 days.

Curly-tails may be induced to breed in indoor terraria by lowering temperatures slightly for a period of about 60 days during midwinter, maintaining a natural photoperiod (short winter days gradually lengthening into the long days of summer), and by an occasional gentle misting during the lengthening days of spring.

Skinks

Description: As a group, skinks are widely distributed throughout many tropical and temperate regions of the world. They vary in size from somewhat more than two feet (61 cm) in length to only a few inches. Most are between five and twelve inches (13–31 cm) in length when adult.

Some of those available in the pet trade are desert species (see pages 104–109), but others will thrive in either dry woodland or savanna terraria.

Skinks enjoy seclusion. Although they may bask openly, they are always ready to scuttle into or beneath ground litter if disturbed. Most are terrestrial, but will climb if necessary. Some are active and agile arborealists.

mainstays of the pet industry. Both of these Hispaniolan natives are a little more slender—and a lot more colorful—than the above. Members of this genus lack femoral pores, but the males of all have hemipenial bulges and are more massive than the females. In some species the sexes are noticeably dichromatic with the males being the more brightly colored.

Keeping: Curly-tails feed upon insects and other arthropods as well as some vegetation and are remarkably hardy as captives. They require dry terraria with a sandy substrate into which they will burrow when frightened or cool. They are adept at darting around on rock surfaces and horizontal logs; the terrarium should be decorated accordingly. All will drink water from a shallow dish.

Breeding: These lizards readily breed in our outdoor cage rings during the spring. During cold weather they are inactive, often remaining

Keeping: We provide most with terraria having a minimum floor space of three feet by two feet (91 cm × 61 cm) with a minimum height of 15 inches (38 cm). In this we place several inches of loose loam on top of which sit a few pieces of flat shale. Over the earthen substrate is scattered one-inch to two-inch (2.5 cm–5.1 cm) thick covering of dried leaves and small dried palm fronds. Several layered rocks or sizable limbs in both horizontal and diagonal positions are incorporated to provide vantage points for the lizards. A low drinking dish is always available. The soil temperature varies from 88°F (31°C) on the warm end to about 75°F (24°C) on the cool end.

Although the fire and the broad-headed skinks discussed below are primarily insectivorous, captives will also eat canned cat food, night-crawlers, crickets, giant mealworms, and some fruit. The blue-tongued and related skinks are far more omnivorous, consuming both animal and plant matter.

Breeding: Winter cooling, during which time photoperiods are also reduced, will induce many, if not most, skink species to breed.

Fire Skinks
Description: The fire skink, *Mochlus fernandi*, is adult at about one foot (30.5 cm) in length. It is one of the most beautifully colored of all skink species—of all lizards, for that matter. The fire skink is of tropical African distribution. The availability of this magnificent creature in the pet trade fluctuates.

Until recently, the fire skink had not been bred in captivity. It is now being bred sparingly, but the vast majority available are wild-collected specimens. These usually harbor several species of endoparasites that need to be identified and eliminated by a reptile-qualified veterinarian.

Keeping: See the discussion of keeping skinks on this page.

Breeding: This species of skink is very difficult to sex. During the breeding season the dorsum

The African fire skink, Mochlus fernandi, is one of the world's most brightly colored lizards.

of reproductively active males becomes suffused with red. Males are also somewhat heavier bodied than females. We have found probing difficult, but accurate, with males probing more deeply than the females. We suggest that probing be done *only* by experienced herpetoculturists.

Breeding techniques for this species are still being honed. The first breeding success came after one herpetoculturist put his animals in nearly total darkness, in their cage, in the cellar on the cold concrete floor (54 to 60°F [12–16°C]), despite the tropical origin of fire skinks. This technique has now worked on numerous occasions for other hobbyists. It may eventually be found that the cycling regimen for the fire skink does not have to be quite this extreme. After being removed from hibernation, the skinks color up and become reproductively active. At that time the russet dorsum of the males becomes suffused with a vermilion blush and the red of the sides intensifies. Females may be distin-

Roused from brumation for this photo, this adult pair of broad-headed skinks, Plestiodon laticeps, *will soon assume much brighter breeding colors.*

guished from males by their proportionately narrower head and slightly less brilliant coloration. Up to eight eggs are reported and at 84°F (29°C) incubation lasts approximately two months.

Broad-headed Skinks

There are three striped skinks found in eastern United States that are superficially quite similar in external appearance. Only one, the big broad-headed skink, *Plestiodon laticeps*, is seen with any regularity in the pet trade.

Description: Broad-headed skinks are beautiful creatures. When they are babies they have shining black bodies, five (or seven) bright yellow longitudinal lines running from head to tail, and electric blue tails. Females tend to retain the juvenile pattern, but with growth, the body color lightens to tan or light brown. The blue of the tail also fades to brown. At adulthood, male broad-heads usually lose their striping, develop a warm olive-brown body and tail, and develop reddish heads. At breeding time, the jowls (temporal area) broaden and the head intensifies in brilliance. At the height of the breeding season the head color of the most dominant male broad-heads becomes an intense fire-orange. At nearly one foot (30.5 cm) in overall length, broad-heads are by far the largest skinks of eastern North America.

Besides being purchased, broad-headed skinks may be field-collected by hobbyists. While size alone will

identify an adult broad-head from the look-alike species, distinguishing subadults can be difficult. For this we recommend that you consult a field guide such as the excellent *Reptiles and Amphibians—Eastern and Central North America* by Roger Conant and Joseph Collins.

Interestingly, the color theme, including the ontogenetic changes, of our eastern skinks is shared by others of the world's skinks. One such is *E. kishinouyei* of Japan.

Keeping: Broad-headed skinks do well as captives. They thrive on vitamin-enhanced insect diets, but will occasionally accept canned cat foods, a pinch of fresh, soft fruit, or flower blossoms as well.

Breeding: Broad-heads are oviparous and females show a degree of instinctive parental interest in their eggs, guarding them throughout the incubation period. They are known to nest communally. Nests containing several dozen eggs have been found in the wild. Individual females can lay more than a dozen eggs.

Provided they are given a modest winter cooling and a reduced photoperiod, broad-headed skinks are not difficult to breed in captivity. This is especially true of specimens originating from Florida, where they undergo less natural seasonal variation than more northern specimens. The eggs are easily incubated in barely dampened sphagnum at 82 to 86°F (28–30°C). The young emerge after about two months of incubation.

Larger Australian Skinks (The Blue-tongued, Spiny, and Related Skinks)

The Tiliquinae, the skink subfamily to which these lizards belong, contains the largest and some of the prettiest and most "outgoing" of the skinks. Collectively, these are viviparous skinks that nourish the developing young through a placenta. In this section we will discuss a few of the blue-tongued skinks (genus *Tiliqua*), the shingle-backed skink, *Tiliqua rugosa*, and the more variable genus *Egernia*. The latter are variously called the spiny, spiny-tailed, king, or major skinks.

With the exception of the shingle-back, these skinks range from difficult to nearly impossible to sex by external cues. On the shingle-back, the tail of the male is proportionately much longer than that of the female.

The alpine form of the blotched blue-tongued skink, Tiliqua nigrolutea, *combines a gentle disposition with an attractive appearance.*

Admittedly this is comparative, but the difference is quite discernible.

Description: Blue-tongue skinks are large (attaining well over one foot [30.5 cm] in length), heavy-bodied lizards with blue tongues. When moving at a moderate pace, they use their short legs but when hurried, they fold their legs against their body and wriggle like snakes.

As of 1996, the genus *Tiliqua* contained six species. (The very closely related shingle-back, currently in the monotypic genus *Trachydosaurus*, may, or may not, be classified as a *Tiliqua*.) All are from Australia, New Guinea, or the surrounding islands. Until recently, *Tiliqua gigas* was the only species known to occur on New Guinea, but a large number of "undescribed forms," dead ringers for species thought to be restricted to Australia, are currently being shipped from New Guinea. It seems probable that the true origin of these lizards is being masked as exportation from Australia is illegal.

There is dichromatism in the eye color of some species and some populations of the blue-tongued skinks. On those that are dichromatic, the iris of the male is deep orange to orange-brown while that of the female is brown. The color difference is most notable when the lizards are reproductively active. Barring this, the only relatively sure method of sexing blue-tongues is to probe them.

Keeping: We have found that the round caging rings in which we now keep these lizards prevents one specimen from being cornered and injured by another. We also have numerous rockpiles in each cage. These serve both as visual barriers and as hiding areas. Blue-tongue skinks eat cat food, some vegetables, many types of fruit, insects, and an occasional pinky.

Breeding: We have very successfully bred two species of blue-tongued skinks and two morphs of Cunningham's skinks for many years. We breed ours colonially, outside, in the caging rings discussed on pages 19–20. Other herpetoculturists have bred them successfully in large indoor savanna terraria.

Because they are less agonistic, we have found eastern and blotched blue-tongued skinks the easiest to work with. But, at times, even these normally placid species can be savagely aggressive. This tendency toward aggressiveness in normally compatible specimens is usually most apparent in sexually active males and heavily gravid females. The latter will often traverse the distance of their ten-foot (305 cm) diameter pen to attack other females or even your shoes when their parturition date is near. When they are attacking, they often inflate their body, open their mouth wide, and loll the startling cobalt blue tongue nearly to the ground.

Breeding usually takes place in March or April in Florida, when the hours of daylight are continuing to lengthen and when the ambient temperatures are beginning to truly warm. A single male may breed one, two, or even more females, and may do so repeatedly over a course of several weeks. Females give birth about 90 days later.

The neonates are immensely aggressive and will quickly cause injury to one another if they are not separated. Growth is rapid and calcium-D_3 supplements should be provided several times weekly. A well-fed eastern blue-tongue loses much of its aggressiveness by the time it has attained half-size and can breed by the time it is a year of age. Blotched blue-tongues seem to mature more slowly and usually do not reproduce until they are a minimum of 18 months of age.

Many hobbyists consider the Alpine form of the blotched blue-tongued skink, *T. nigrolutea*, the prettiest of the group. Certainly, with its paired blotches of peach or orange, it ranks high in this respect.

The lowland from of the blotched blue-tongue is less contrastingly colored. Of the two forms, the Alpine is larger. Although this skink species is reportedly a biennial breeder in the wild, females may bear two to six, four-inch-long (10.2 cm) young each year.

The eastern blue-tongue, *T. s. scincoides*, is gray with reddish-brown crossbands. A dark postorbital bar is prominent on this 14-inch (36 cm) lizard. Kept communally in outdoor pens, the eastern blue tongues live peacefully, even at breeding time. Females have very large litters of 10 to 22 babies, which grow very rapidly and must receive vitamin and mineral supplements.

The northern blue-tongue. *T. s. intermedia*, is slightly larger than the eastern form. It has no postorbital bar, and bears peach-colored lateral blotches that are much brighter than its dorsal bands. When housed communally, the northern blue-tongues squabble to the point of removing each others' toes and tailtips. Females have smaller litters than the easterns, with just five to twelve in a clutch. Babies are even crabbier than the adults, and survive best if kept singly. They also need vitamin and mineral supplements.

The Papuan/New Guinean blue-tongue, *T. gigas*, is a quarrelsome species that may grow to 18 inches (45.7 cm). It is generally inexpensive, at least in America. Females

Shingle-backed (or stump-tailed) skinks, Tiliqua rugosa, *are normally gentle lizards that need an arid environment to thrive.*

areas. They do best in outdoor caging where temperatures and humidity levels allow. Parturition may be either annual or biennial. The females give birth to one or two immense babies.

Spiny and Spiny-tailed Skinks

Egernia, a genus of skinks closely allied to the blue-tongues, are also primarily of Australian distribution. One, the large *E. frerei*, occurs also in New Guinea. Of the total of 30 plus species, only a handful are captive bred outside of Australia. Like the blue-tongues, exportation of these lizards from Australia is prohibited.

Although these small to very large skinks can be bred in indoor terraria, they seem to breed best when kept in naturalistic settings out of doors.

Perhaps the best-known "species" of this group is the Australian Cunningham's skink, *E. cunninghami*. It appears that the variably colored lizards we now refer to as *E. cunninghami* are actually a complex of several species. At the very least, the species contains several well-defined morphs.

Description: The scales of these robust, spiny lizards are heavily keeled. The spines are best developed and most prominent on the tail. Cunningham's skinks are fairly large lizards, usually topping out at 12 inches (30.5 cm), but occasionally attaining 16 inches (41 cm) in total length. The tail and body are of roughly equal length.

give birth to six to twelve agonistic babies, which will survive unscarred only if kept singly. Like those of the other blue-tongues, the babies of this species also grow rapidly and need vitamin and mineral supplementation.

The shingle-back skink, *Tiliqua rugosa*, is a denizen of very dry savannas or desert habitat. In appearance, the shingle-back looks like a foot-long (30.5 cm), animated pine cone. Also called the stump-tailed skink, this big (to 16 inches [41 cm]) lizard is covered with very large scales. It is some shade of dark brown with intermittent white scales.

Those brought into humid areas will do well for a year or so, and then decline. Indoor, low humidity quarters are necessary to even attempt to keep this lizard long-term in humid areas.

Shingle-backs thrive and have even been bred when kept in arid

Keeping: Cunningham's skinks are omnivores, but seem to prefer canned cat food and insects to vegetation. These are long-lived lizards, with some records exceeding fifteen years.

Cunningham's skinks live well in colonies. If cages are large and have sufficient visual barriers (rock piles or logs) more than one male may be kept per cage. In smaller cages, however, a colony of one male and several females seems best.

Breeding: This is not an easily sexed species. Probing *may* help, but we have not found this method to be conclusive. This was brought graphically home to us when a long-term specimen that we thought to be a large and robust male, gave birth one summer to a clutch of healthy babies!

Cunningham's skinks are easily bred. Normal clutch size varies from two to six large babies. Larger, older females produce the larger clutches, both in number and neonate size.

All of our many breeding successes with Cunningham's skinks have occurred in our outdoor cages. Others have bred them in large indoor cages (approximate floor space of 4 feet × 8 feet [122 cm × 244 cm]). The seasonal fluctuations of temperature and photoperiod normally associated with reproductive cycling seem to work well with Cunningham's skinks.

Description: Perhaps the most attractive of the *Egernia* is the pygmy spiny tail, *E. depressa*. Short and

Cunningham's skinks, Egernia cunninghami, *occur in several color phases.*

compact, with a broad, depressed tail, the pygmy spiny tail varies from a warm gray (more or less splotched or banded with terra cotta) to terra cotta with occasional splotches of gray. The dorsal and lateral scales are strongly keeled, and the tail scales bear three keels. The entire lizard bristles like a scrub brush. It is adult at from about 4.5 inches to 6 inches (11 cm–15 cm) in overall length. Male *E. depressa* have a pro-

The Major skink, Egernia frerei, *is large, active, and rather attractive.*

portionately longer, narrower tail than that of the female.

Keeping: Although originally from rocky outcroppings and termitaria in desert areas of western Australia, captives do not seem adversely affected by high humidity.

Breeding: We have bred this species on only two occasions, once under entirely "natural" conditions outside in one of our cage rings (see pages 19–20) and once under more regimented conditions in an indoor terrarium. The indoor lizards were subjected to the normal winter cooling and reduction of photoperiod. Breeding occurred from mid-March to mid-April and parturition occurred in late June. The *depressa* in the outside container gave birth to only a single baby; those indoors produced two. Up to three babies have been recorded.

Egernia frerei, the Major skink, is from eastern Australia, New Guinea, and a few islands in the Torres Strait.

Description: These lizards are tan to buff, often with a dark longitudinal dash on each of the dorsal scales. At a distance, these dashes give the impression of a striped lizard. The scales are keeled but not spiny. Larger specimens near 18 inches (46 cm) in total length, with the tapering tail being about 125 percent of the body length.

Keeping: Captive specimens are not picky feeders, eating cat food, vegetation, baby mice, and crickets.

Breeding: This is not an easy species to sex. When grasped, frightened males will often evert their hemipenes. If this occurs, the sex is obvious. If it doesn't, though, one must wonder whether one has a male that hasn't everted or a female. Gentle probing has been used with success. Females have a narrower head than the male, and except when gravid, are less massive in overall build.

Although we never witnessed breeding, our female gave birth to three large babies in mid-January. Since this coincides more nearly to parturition times in the southern hemisphere than in the north, it is possible (even probable) that this female was gravid when collected and imported.

After becoming acclimated to the reversed progression of seasons in the northern hemisphere (this, like all tiliquines, is a southern hemisphere lizard), *E. frerei* has been bred in captivity. Breeding has been induced by subjecting the lizards to the normal regimen of winter care

The snail-eating pink-tongued skink, **Hemisphaerodon gerrardi,** *a creature of evening and nighttime activity, can be difficult to acclimate to more readily available diets.*

(slight cooling, reduced humidity and lessened photoperiod). Breeding then occurs in March, April, and early May with parturition occurring some 85 to 100 days later.

The Specialized Pink-tongued Skink

Description: Until recently *Hemisphaerodon gerrardi*, the single species in this genus, was considered a member of the larger genus *Tiliqua*. It is a slender species, the adults of which develop massively enlarged heads.

Keeping: Although in nature this is a specialized slug and snail feeder, most captives will rather readily accept fish-flavored (and occasionally other) cat foods. Pink-tongued skinks are not adversely impacted by high humidity.

Breeding: The pink-tongued skink is extensively bred by both American and European hobbyists, although it is difficult to sex individual specimens. Probing may be inconclusive.

Although a winter cooling (not hibernation!) and shortened day length will certainly help with reproductive cycling, such preparation is not always necessary to successfully breed this warmth-loving, lowland species. They live fairly well in groups, although an occasional male may become aggressive.

The clutches of this live-bearing skink are large, numbering up to as many as 25 slender, big-headed babies. The neonates are clad in neat, precise bands of bright tan and black. A broad black subocular blotch is also present. With growth, the ground color fades to gray and the dark bands are invaded with lighter pigment. The cranial scales usually have dark sutures. Some very old males may lose much of the dark pigmentation. Although most specimens are smaller, a total length of more than 18 inches (46 cm) is attained by some. The prehensile tail, a somewhat curious adaptation for a basically terrestrial lizard, is long, usually being at least 130 percent of the SVL.

Alligator and Glass Lizards

Anguids are elongate lizards that superficially resemble snakes—until they begin to move. The awkward, clumsy, broadly S-shaped curves employed in the movement tells any observer that this is no snake.

The reason for the stiffness is the presence of osteoderms (tiny bony plates beneath the scales). The osteoderms offer protection, much as a suit of armor does, but at the price of mobility.

Some anguids are legless (glass lizards and slow worms), while others have weak legs (alligator and diploglossine lizards). The legged forms include some strong climbers and some non-climbers.

Many anguids have weakly prehensile tails, and all have functional eyelids and ear openings. Most have a longitudinal, expandable

The Eurasian giant glass lizard or sheltopusik, Ophisaurus apodus, *is the largest of the anguid lizards and is often available to hobbyists. Most are brown but a few are mottled like the pictured adult.*

fold on each side to provide extra room during respiration and when the lizards ingest sizable meals.

The largest member of the genus is the European glass lizard, *Ophisaurus apodus*. Nearly four feet (122 cm) in length, it can be found in the U.S. pet trade as *scheltopusik*, a German name.

Breeding: Although anguids are not frequently bred in captivity, with proper cycling this is easily accomplished. If their quarters are cooled—52 to 58°F (11–14°C)—and darkened in the winter months for a period of from 60 to 75 days, during which time water should be available but food is not necessary, when warmed again, adult anguids will progress through the physiological changes required to enable breeding to take place. They should be heavily fed when warmed, and the females given additional calcium to help with egg yolk and eggshell development.

If you are able to provide suitable warmth and moisture, the eggs may be left with the female for their entire incubation period. If your facility does not provide for this the eggs may be removed and incubated as you would snake eggs. We have successfully incubated the eggs of several anguid species at 82 to 88°F (27.8–31°C); 84 to 86°F (28.9–30°C) seems best for most.

Unlike the alligator lizard group that contains both egg-laying and live-bearing reproductive modes, all of the glass lizards (genus *Ophisaurus*) are egg layers. The normal clutch size for all larger specimens seems to number about a dozen, although some clutches may be considerably larger. Incubation durations that we have observed have varied from as little as 43 to as many as 65 days. Females remain with their clutches, coiled around them.

Slow Worm

The single species of slow worm, *Anguis fragilis*, is the only member of its genus and of the subfamily Anguinae.

Description: This interesting, rather small, ovoviviparous species is well known by European herpetoculturists but not often seen in American herp circles.

Its range includes most of mainland Europe, Great Britain, southwest Asia, and northwest Africa. The slow worm is prone to desiccation, so tends to stay in moist surroundings. Although slow worms may bask and thermoregulate in the open at times, more frequently they choose to thermoregulate beneath sun-warmed boards, roofing tins, or other such cover.

The slow worm is clad in smooth, shiny scales of reddish-brown, brown, gray, or silvery gray. Males tend to be unicolored; females often have darker sides and a dark vertebral stripe (which may be absent posteriorly). The neonates are bright silver or silver-buff, often with at least vestiges of a middorsal stripe and with dark sides and venter.

Adult male slow worms with original tails may attain a length in excess of 16 inches (40.6 cm) but most are considerably smaller. The tail is somewhat greater in length than the SVL. Although the tail breaks rather easily, its regeneration capabilities are poor at best.

Keeping: Although it seems that the slow worms' favorite food item is slugs, the lizards also consume earthworms, centipedes, and other such secretive creatures. Slow worms are long lived—at least in captivity, where a longevity of more than five decades has been recorded.

Breeding: See general discussion of breeding Anguid lizards, page 130.

Alligator Lizards

Description: There are hardly any lizards more adept at remaining out of sight than the lizards of the genera *Gerrhonotus* (and *Elgaria*). Although considerable numbers may be present in a given area, they normally remain beneath leaf litter and other

Supplemental vitamin D₃ and calcium additives seem mandatory for success with the Texas alligator lizard, Gerrhonotus infernalis.

debris. Surprisingly, large individuals are able to conceal themselves behind small shards of loosened bark, beneath rocks, logs, or trash. A favored site, especially during periods of drought, is inside decomposing, moisture-retaining tree trunks.

None of the alligator lizards are brightly colored, all being clad in browns and grays, often with darker markings.

Alligator lizards of several kinds occur in the western United States and Mexico. The young of many forms are prominently crossbanded. Both the southern, *E. multicarinatus*, and the Texas, *G. infernalis*, are seen in the pet trade.

During cool weather and at high elevations, alligator lizards tend toward diurnal activity. As the daytimes warm, the lizards indulge in both crepuscular and nocturnal activity patterns. Although they are often found in rather arid areas, alligator lizards are most common

Most examples of the various subspecies of northern alligator lizard are brown but some develop yellow highlights during the breeding season. A Shasta alligator lizard, Elgaria coerulea shastensis, *is pictured.*

insects and other arthropods, newly born mice, smaller lizards, and tiny snakes. Some captives will lap up eggs and accept high-quality canned cat foods. Vitamin/mineral supplements should be added. Metabolic bone disease was noted in a long-term captive specimen that was sent to us. Injected liquid calcium was sufficient to reverse the progression of this condition, and supplemental D_3 and powdered calcium additives were a part of future feedings. In the several years that we kept him, the problem never reoccurred.

Breeding: Of the commonly seen alligator lizards, only the several subspecies of the northern, *G. coeruleus* ssp., are ovoviviparous. Large females annually produce single clutches of about a dozen babies. The number of eggs produced by the others is variable—up to about a dozen by the small Madrean species and more than 30 by the larger species. Females usually remain with their clutches; we have been told that a disturbed female on the nest site will bite, but have always left them alone.

Glass Lizards

Of the four American species of glass lizards, it is the eastern, *O. ventralis*, that is seen most often in the pet trade. This species can tolerate more dampness than the others.

Of the four U.S. glass lizard species, three have fracture planes (weakened breaking points) in their caudal vertebrae, and readily autotomize and regenerate their tails.

near water sources. Some are rather agile climbers, using their partially prehensile tail to assist them in maintaining secure holds while aloft.

Keeping: Alligator lizards make hardy captives, and because of their short legs are not prone to making fast dashes into the sides of their terraria. As a matter of fact, unless severely stressed they seem to study all moves they make thoroughly, including hunting insect prey. After perceiving a vulnerable insect, an alligator lizard approaches it slowly and steadily, sneaking in, rather than dashing, for the attack. When close enough, it rears its head back (often lifting its neck and forebody as well), and then darts the head forward with powerful jaws agape. Seldom does the lizard miss its target.

In captivity, alligator lizards need a dry substrate and always must be provided with clean, fresh water. Bark pieces or other such cover should be liberally provided. Diet can include

Slender glass lizards, (*O. attenuatus* ssp.), for instance, are both nervous and active and will often autotomize their tail with even the gentlest of handling. Although it will quickly regenerate, the loss can prove more than a little disconcerting to even the most cautious and stalwart collector. Only the island glass lizard, (*O. compressus*), lacks both the fracture planes and the ability to readily regrow its tail. If broken, the tail of this latter species regenerates slowly and often incompletely.

The genus *Ophisaurus* is well represented in Europe, Mexico, and Asia as well.

Of the American anguids it is the eastern glass lizard, Ophisaaurus ventralis *(of the southeastern United States), that is most often seen in the pet trade.*

Description: The European glass lizard (or scheltopusik), *O. apodus*, is a magnificent, heavy-bodied beast that is clad in keeled scales of warm brown on all but the head, which is pale. At four feet (122 cm) in length, it is the largest species of the family. It is popular with both American and European hobbyists. Despite being kept in fair numbers, it has been bred only a few times. It is quite resistant to desiccation and often inhabits rather dry areas. It ranges widely through the Balkan countries as well as occurring in southwest Asia and North Africa. Unlike those of many of its relatives, the tail of this species does not break easily, nor when it does break, is regeneration complete.

Recently, small numbers of the little slow worm lookalike, *O. formosensis*, have been showing up in the American pet trade. Those that

we have seen have been about 14 inches (36 cm) in total length. The two that we had eagerly ate small slugs and small earthworms but refused crickets and mealworms.

Keeping: The large size of the adult scheltopusik makes it a fearsome predator. Captives readily eat all manner of insects and arthropods and can quickly overpower and consume fair-sized mice. They will usually also eat canned cat foods, but these should be offered in limited quantities.

Captive lifespans of more than 20 years are not uncommon.

If kept properly, the glass lizards make satisfactory, long-lived captives. They even become used to gentle handling, with the huge *Ophisaurus apodus* actually seeming to enjoy attention. On a diet of vitamin and mineral-enhanced insects, pinky mice, an occasional treat of beaten egg yolk and high-quality canned cat food, glass lizards will thrive for years. Both bark shards for cover and a dry substrate (sand is perfect) into which they can burrow should be provided for these creatures. Clean, fresh drinking water should always be present.

Hatchlings of this egg-laying species are quite pale and have prominent dark dorsal barring.

Girdle-tailed Lizards and Relatives

Of the cordylids, only three genera are regularly seen in the pet market. All are African. These include some of the smaller girdle-tailed lizards *Cordylus*, one or two species each of crag lizard, *Pseudocordylus*, and one of the flattened rock lizards, *Platysaurus*.

Description: The cordylids are of variable conformation and equally variable habitat, and, depending on the species, range in size from four to eighteen inches (10.2–45.7 cm).

These are flat-bodied lizards, well adapted to life in rocky crags. Body depression is carried to the extreme in the various flattened rock lizards of the genus *Platysaurus*. Flattening is less pronounced on the relatively gigantic, burrow-digging sungazer.

Keeping: Although the bulk of the diet of most species involves insects and other arthropods, some of the larger forms eat nestling rodents and may even consume a fair amount of vegetation in the form of blossoms or tender leaves. Captive cordylids will drink from water dishes, but more eagerly lap up water droplets on the rocks of their enclosures.

As a group, the cordylids are adapted to hot, dry, low-humidity habitats. Many of the species are subjected to considerable seasonal and daily (day-night) temperature variations. Many of the species of *Cordylus* regularly thermoregulate to elevate body temperatures to more than 103°F (39°C). The rock surfaces in our outside pens were often close to 115°F (46°C), and were favored basking areas for our cordylids.

If provided with ample room, dry conditions, and adequate food and water supply and areas of concealment, most cordylids will thrive as captives. Most are not aggressively territorial, coexisting well in mixed-sex groups. At least one species, the armadillo lizard, *Cordylus cataphrac-*

Although the exact species has not yet been ascertained, this attractive little girdle-tailed lizard, Cordylus sp., *was collected in Tanzania.*

tus, is known to exist peacefully in family groups, even after sexual maturity is reached by the young.

Breeding: Few of these hardy species have been captive bred and of these efforts, the most successful seem to have been by herpetoculturists in South Africa. It is probable that photoperiod plays an immensely important role and that temperature manipulation would also be beneficial, especially for the less tropical species.

The Sungazer

Description: The most impressive of all cordylids is the big, heavily armored sungazer, *C. giganteus.* This terrestrial 13-inch-long (33 cm) species lives communally and digs long (to five feet [152 cm]) home burrows.

The tail of this species fairly bristles with enlarged, heavily keeled scales. The occipital spines are enlarged and spinose. The dorsal and neck scales are also spinose, more prominently so paravertebrally and dorsolaterally.

Although not brightly colored, the overall earthen tones of this lizard are pleasing. The brown of the dorsum shades to yellowish laterally. The throat and venter are quite a bright yellow or cream.

When threatened, the sungazer dives headfirst into its burrow and swats approaching predators with its powerful tail. If forcible removal from its burrow is attempted, the sungazer tilts its snout downward and raises its head, thus anchoring itself with its occipital spines.

Keeping: Captive lifespans well in excess of 20 years have been recorded.

Breeding: Although this species is notoriously difficult to breed in captivity it is very hardy and easily kept. One or two 5.5-inch (14 cm) young are born.

Armadillo Lizards

Description: The little (4.5 inch to 6.5 inch [11 cm–16.5 cm]) *C. tropidosternum* is commonly available in the pet trades of America and Europe. The nominate form *C. t. tropidosternum* is generally called the tropical girdle-tailed or "armadillo" lizard, while its smaller southern race, *C. t. jonesi,* is called Jones' armadillo lizard.

The South African sungazer or giant girdle-tailed lizard, Cordylus giganteus, *has proven easy to maintain but very difficult to breed.*

Two very pretty girdle-tailed lizards of moderate size are C. polyzonus, *the Karoo girdle-tail (top), and* C. mozambicus, *the orange-sided girdle-tail (bottom). Both are occasionally available to hobbyists.*

C. t. tropidosternum is tan to brick in ground color while *C. t. jonesi* is olive gray. Light vertebral markings and darker smudgings may or may not be present. This species is a dweller on trees and logs where it finds protection beneath exfoliating bark.

Keeping: These lizards feed on insects and other arthropods; our captives seemed to prefer termites over any other insect.

Breeding: Armadillo lizards are ovoviviparous, bearing from two to four young.

The Warren's Armadillo Lizard Group

Description: The several sub-species of *C. warreni* are quietly colored yet attractive and hardy. Up to 11 inches (30.5 cm) in overall length, the several subspecies can be differentiated by the number and comparative size of the occipital spines, as well as by color and overall pattern.

These wary lizards are rock-crevice dwellers and agile and strong predators. They eat not only insects and other arthropods, but small vertebrates as well.

Keeping: Wild-caught adults of this species have frequently lived more than five years as captives and some have neared a decade. Under ideal conditions, it seems likely that captive lifespans in excess of 15 years could be attained.

Breeding: From one to six live babies are produced annually.

Flat Lizards (also called Flattened Rock Lizards)

Description: The 10+/− members of this genus (*Platysaurus*) are so flattened that in some cases they appear two dimensional. Males in breeding dress are gaudily garbed in greens, russets, blues, tans, and yellows, variable by species and most brilliant ventrally. Some males avoid actual skirmishes by flashing the ventral colors during territorial disputes. The tail (usually bright red-orange) is often of distinctively different color than the body. The females are dark, usually black or olive dorsally (lighter laterally) with three thin yellow longitudinal lines. When not in breeding colors, males can also be dark, but usually not as dark as the females.

The body scales are small, granular, and not arranged in regular rows. There is no evidence of spinosity other than on the tail where the enlarged scales form regular whorls.

These remarkable lizards are dwellers of exfoliating crags. Where conditions are ideal, sizable populations may be encountered.

Breeding: Unlike the other members of this subfamily, *Platysaurus* is oviparous, producing a pair of eggs. Communal nesting is well documented.

Seen most often in the American pet trade are the various subspecies of the common flat lizard, *P. intermedius*. They were once much more readily available to herpetoculturists than they now are. Depending on the subspecies, the dorsal color of the males can vary from light golden tan (*wilhelmi*) through reddish-brown (*rhodesianus*) to bright green (*natalensis* and *intermedius*). Light dots or reticulations are present and vertebral and/or dorsolateral lines may be present. If so, they are often best defined anteriorly. The tails of all are russet. The ventral color is as variable as the dorsal, ranging from brilliant blue to reddish.

Plated Lizards and Zonosaurs

Although they are not as eagerly sought as the members of the cordylidae, many of the gerrhosaurid lizards are more readily available. This is especially true of the several species of *Gerrhosaurus* and numerous species of *Zonosaurus*. Not only are they readily available, but, at the moment, they are inexpensive as well.

Description: Some generalities about the members of this family: All have a heavy, regular scalation with each scale underlain by an osteoderm and, except for the attenuate members of the genus *Tetradactylus*, all have sturdy, functional limbs. Many of the species bear a lateral fold of skin (similar to the New World alligator lizards). This is most prominently visible on the lower sides of

The emperor flat lizard, Platysaurus imperator, *is a large and pretty member of this crevice-dwelling genus.*

Gerrhosaurus major, the rough-scaled plated lizard, is the most commonly seen of the large gerrhosaurs.

the neck and anterior body. Most of the plated lizards are of robust build and not at all flattened.

Keeping: In addition to insects, many of the larger members of this subfamily will consume seeds, dried leaves, blossoms, and some succulent vegetation. When being maintained as captives, offer them a wide variety of foods. Many captive specimens will consume canned cat and dog foods as well as an array of fruits and vegetables.

Breeding: All are oviparous.

African Plated Lizards

The plated lizards are widely distributed in suitable habitats from central Africa southward. They are easily

kept and long-lived lizards. A captive lifespan of a decade or more can be expected from even wild-caught adults. All avidly consume insects and other arthropods. The larger forms also eat nestling rodents, birds, blossoms, and other vegetation. The captives of many species may also be offered fruit and limited quantities of canned cat and dog foods. Fresh water should always be available.

G. major is the plated lizard best known to American hobbyists. It ranges widely in savanna land over much of central eastern Africa. Its common name, "rough-scaled plated lizard," aptly describes the heavily keeled dorsal and dorso-lateral scales.

Description: *G. major* is a robust lizard that attains a size of 18 inches (45.7 cm) or more. The tail is flattened basally but rounded and tapering distally. It is rather a unicolored olive-tan to olive-gray dorsally and laterally and lighter ventrally. The dorsal scales may, or may not, have dark centers. When the dark centers are present they often impart the overall appearance of a striped lizard. The chin and throat are usually the brightest parts of this lizard. In color these areas vary from nearly white to yellow, peach, or in some northern populations, blue. The throat of male specimens may be more brightly colored than those of females, especially in breeding season.

The yellow-throated plated lizard, Gerrhosaurus flavigularis, is small of body and long of tail.

Breeding: Without really knowing it was happening, we found that this species bred on several occasions in our large open-air enclosures. Although we neither saw evidence of breeding nor found the eggs, several babies were seen late each summer. The babies were close to five inches (12.7 cm) in length when first seen.

This is a very hardy species that has been captive bred only a few times. Tremendous numbers are imported for the pet markets and if properly cared for, a longevity of 15 or more years can be expected.

Zonosaurs or Malagasy Smooth-scaled Plated Lizards

The island nation of Madagascar is currently undergoing a herpetological renaissance. New species, even an occasional new genus, are now regularly being found. The gerrhosaurid genus *Zonosaurus* has certainly not been omitted from the new finds. To the three species assigned to this genus only a few years ago, another ten have been added.

Description: As of March 1995 a total of 13 zonosaurs are known. Many are of rather similar appearance, differing in the number or placement of light dorsal or dorsolateral stripes, but others are of dramatically different color and pattern and remarkably beautiful. Six, and occasionally one or two more, zonosaur species now appear regularly on dealers' lists.

As a group, the zonosaurs are basically terrestrial, tropical lizards. They occur in varied habitats. Some,

The Malagasy members of the family Gerrhosauridae are contained in the genus Zonosaurus. *This is the four-lined plated lizard,* Z. quadrilineatus.

clearing and forest edge dwellers, may bask extensively. Others, dwellers of the forest itself or cooler riverine areas, enjoy warm temperatures but seldom bask.

Keeping: Now that they are available, the longevity records of many are quickly accruing. Many have already survived for more than five years in captivity and it is expected that with the passing of time records of 10, 15, or even 20 years will occur. We have kept several species and have found all remarkably undemanding. All fed readily on insects, anellids, various fruits, and canned cat and dog foods. Captives thrive when given spacious quarters with both full-spectrum and basking lights available should they choose to partake. Daytime temperatures are in the area of 77 to 90°F (25–32°C). Nighttime temperatures drop somewhat but not radically. As might be expected, the specimens kept outside bask most extensively after cool nights.

The tails of most are about one and a half times the SVL. The heads of most are rather narrow and the snouts are rather sharply pointed.

The olive-brown dorsum of the 14-inch-long (35.6 cm) *Z. madagascariensis* is separated from the darker lateral areas by a broad yellow dorsolateral line on each side. The dorsolateral lines are best defined anteriorly. The lateral fold is often edged dorsally with reddish scales. This species is often called the two-striped zonosaur. This is a common species that adapts well to disturbed, even degraded, areas.

The largest member of the genus is the big—to 27 inches (69 cm)—long-tailed (200 percent of SVL) giant zonosaur, *Z. maximus*. This is a dark species with very vague to absent dorsolateral lines. The males are the larger sex and have a suffusion of orange along the sides from the rear of the jaw to the hind legs.

Z. haraldmeieri, the green zonosaur, is a beautiful species of moderate size—to 14 inches (36 cm). The flanks are grayish green,

the dorsum a greenish gray (both are suffused with rather regularly arranged dark fleckings) and a wash of orange is usually present on the snout. Dorsolateral stripes are lacking. In our estimation, this is the prettiest member of the genus and one of the most attractive species in the entire family.

Breeding: Similar to the continental members of this family, the zonosaurs are proving difficult to breed in captivity but despite this are remarkably hardy. All are oviparous.

Lacertid Lizards

Jeweled and Green Lacertas
Description: The eyed or jeweled lizard, *Timon lepidus*, is the largest member of the genus *Lacerta*. With a total length of 18 inches to 32 inches (45.7 cm–81 cm), two-thirds of which is tail, this is a fair-sized lizard. Males become very bulky and broad-headed with advancing age.

In coloration the eyed lizard is green to gray-green both dorsally and laterally. The dorsum is sparsely to heavily overlain with black reticulations. A series of lateral, brilliant blue ocelli give this species its common name. Females are often paler and smaller than the males. The hatchlings are also paler than the males and are usually strongly patterned both dorsally and laterally with dark-edged light ocelli.

In the wilds of the Iberian Peninsula and adjacent France and

The largest member of the family Lacertidae is the pretty-eyed lizard, Timon lepidus.

extreme northeastern Italy, these lizards prefer dry, open woodlands and scrub but may also be seen quite close to human habitations. They are very wary and not at all easily approached. They calm down in captivity, and the eyed lacerta becomes quite placid.

Keeping: The diet of the jeweled lizard changes with maturity. Hatchlings eat small insects. Adults broaden their tastes to include small rodents, nestling birds, arachnids such as scorpions and solpugids (also called sun "spiders"), smaller lizards, and some fruit and blossoms. Well-maintained captive jeweled lizards have survived for more than 20 years.

Jeweled lizards need large cages with room to dash about. They require a well-lit heated basking area, and vitamin- and mineral-enhanced food. Captives drink copiously from water dishes.

All of the members of this genus do quite well in captivity. Some species have been known to live more than 10 years in captivity, some near 15; a few have been kept for more than 20 years. Dust food items with calcium-D_3 supplements, especially for growing babies.

L. viridis is often referred to as the common green lizard, an apt name. Adult males, especially those that are reproductively active, often have a blue throat and females and juveniles have either two or four light body lines. A vertebral line is lacking. This species will reach a foot or more (30.5 cm) in length. It is widely distributed in Europe.

Schrieber's (or Spanish) green lizard, *L. schreiberi*, occurs on the Iberian Peninsula. Adult males tend to have numerous slightly darker spots dorsally and females are usually brownish with dark paravertebral and flank spots. Both females and males reach a foot (30.5 cm) in length, with the males being larger.

Another large, alert and active member of this group is the very attractive *L. jayakeri*. This sought-after lizard is slender and hardy. The dorsal and lateral surfaces of this Arabian lizard are slate to terra cotta, profusely patterned with dark and light reticulations. This species attains a length of 18 inches (45.7 cm). Adult specimens will eat insects, arthropods, nestling birds, young rodents, and some vegetation.

Breeding: Many species of lacertids are kept and bred as terrarium inhabitants. The smaller members of this lizard family are especially popular with European hobbyists. American hobbyists are

Very popular with European hobbyists, few of the lacertid lizards have found favor with American enthusiasts. This is a male European green lizard, Lacerta viridis.

partial to the large and/or brilliantly colored species.

It seems that all lacertids require some variation of the regimen of cycling discussed on pages 58–59 to attain reproductive readiness. The degree of winter cooling required varies according to the origin of the animals, with those from the more northerly regions and higher altitudes needing cooler winter temperatures for a longer duration than lizards from the south or from low altitudes.

Adult males are often quite agonistic to others of their sex, and are especially so during the breeding season. Males may also injure non-receptive females during breeding attempts. At this time, the interactions of the lizards should be watched closely. Properly cycled females may indicate their breeding readiness by arm waving (circumduction).

We have successfully bred several species both in large outside cages and in rather spacious indoor facilities. A floor space of 2.5 × 4 feet was provided for a colony of one male and three female eyed lizards. Smaller species would require somewhat less space. Besides a large, flat dish of water, the cage contained a nearly dry earth, limbs and several areas of seclusion in the form of flat boards lying atop the substrate. The boards were warmed from above by 50w floodlights and the lizards often would sprawl and bask atop them. The lacertids burrowed beneath the flat boards persistently. They would retire beneath the boards for the night and it was there that the females would deposit their clutches of from four to a dozen eggs.

The eggs were incubated at moderate humidity at a temperature that varied from 82–85°F. Hatchlings emerged after about two and a half months of incubation. It has been suggested by very knowledgeable European breeders that incubation temperatures above 86°F result in weakened hatchlings or actual embryo death.

Frilled Lizards and Bearded Dragons

Frilled Lizards

Description: The frilled lizard is a big (to 32 inches [81.3 cm], two-thirds of which is tail) lizard of the dry northern Australian and southern Papuan/New Guinean woodlands. *Chlamydosaurus kingi* is best known for the large frill on the neck, which is erected when startled or displaying. In natural habitat the lizard is often seen clinging to the trunks of a tree, perched jauntily atop an anthill or termite mound or high up on other elevated points. Frilled lizards may display while clinging vertically to a tree trunk.

These lizards are semiarboreal, readily climbing into the canopy, yet are equally adept at running. They employ a fast bipedal style when hard-pressed. Like other agamids, their front teeth are fanglike.

Until very recently this big agamid was a rarity in Europe and America, seen only in zoological gardens. In the early 1990s, however, several hundred specimens were imported from Irian Jaya and quickly sold. Those accustomed to the nervous behaviors of larger lizards were a little apprehensive about these new captives, but frilled lizards have proven hardy and unexpectedly quiet. In fact, the frilled lizards acclimated so completely that it became difficult to induce them to display their frill.

As with many lizards, adult male frilled lizards are of a more massive build than adult females. Males also have larger femoral and preanal pores and a hemipenial bulge at the tail base.

Keeping: Although strongly insectivorous, frilled lizards also consume nestling birds and rodents and other lizards. Small specimens readily drink the vitamin enhanced fruit-honey mixture provided for day geckos (see page 164 for formula). Frilled lizards drink droplets on leaves and limbs and from shallow dishes. During hot weather they seem to enjoy clambering into a water receptacle large and deep enough for them to submerge.

It is difficult to ascribe an indoor terrarium size to such a large active lizard species. While babies would do well for a while in terraria 20 to 30 gallons (75.7–114 L) in size, we feel that even a 75 to 100 gallon (284–378.5 L) terrarium would seriously constrain a pair of adults.

Although frilled lizards may be inactive for long periods, like other agamids they move quickly when

Once a rarely seen lizard outside of its native Australia and New Guinea, the spectacular frilled lizard, Chlamydosaurus kingi, *is now bred by many hobbyists worldwide.*

startled. Because they exist in a vertical habitat as well as a horizontal one, cages must provide sufficient space in both planes. Adequate elevated areas and visual barriers will be important in helping this lizard feel secure.

Breeding: Frilled lizards are oviparous. Gravid females have laid 4 to 15 eggs in the corners of their cages. We feel under outdoor conditions the females would dig a burrow for egg deposition. Those kept in spacious facilities in California, Texas, and Florida have bred. Breeding activity has occurred in the spring and early summer. Reproductive activity seems as much stimulated by the advent of the seasonal summer rains as by lengthened photoperiod and higher average temperatures.

Bearded Dragons

Description: The bearded dragons are named for the enlarged, conical scales in the gular area

Inland bearded dragons, Pogona vitticeps, *have taken the hobby by storm. Selective breeding has enhanced the richness of color and patterns of these Australian lizards.*

that form the appearance of beards, although not all of the species have beards. They are heavy-bodied and quietly attractive Australian endemics. They have a quiet and confiding nature and seem unafraid and very responsive to their keepers. At least four of the seven (or eight) species in the genus *Pogona* are captive bred in some numbers. The most popular member of the genus is *P. vitticeps*, one of the larger species, which is now captive bred in tremendous numbers both in America and Europe.

As a group, bearded dragons are heliothermic (sun-basking), heat-tolerant lizards. Body temperatures of basking lizards may exceed 95°F (35°C). During cold periods, dragons become reclusive and inactive. Although often seen on the ground, bearded dragons easily climb fence posts, dead trees, anthills, and other such elevated positions to bask and display. The most dominant males

usually assume the most prominent positions. A curious arm-waving (circumduction), exhibited by both young and adults, apparently acts as an appeasement gesture. The gesture is used particularly often by subadult and adult female lizards.

The smaller species are primarily insectivorous but the larger forms are quite omnivorous.

Keeping: Bearded dragons seem prone to calcium metabolism disorders. Be certain that the calcium/phosphorus ratios are at least 2:1 in favor of calcium and that sufficient D_3 is provided to permit calcium absorbtion and metabolism.

Breeding: The beards are distended for territorial displays and during the breeding season. The throats of the males darken as the breeding season nears. All bearded dragons are oviparous.

P. barbatus, the eastern bearded dragon, is marginally the largest species. It may reach a length of 22 inches (56 cm); just over half the length is tail. This is generally the species darkest in coloration, with some almost a charcoal ground color. Other specimens may have a ground color of buff or sand-red. Enlarged, conical spines adorn the beard of this species, making the breeding display especially impressive. The mouth is opened as part of the display, its lining of bright to mustard yellow an impressive sight. Although eastern bearded dragons are occasionally available to hobbyists, they are considered a little more difficult to keep and breed than the more commonly seen inland bearded dragon, *P. vitticeps*.

Despite this, because it is adapted to habitats along Australia's relatively humid east coast, the eastern bearded dragon might be the best choice for hobbyists located in humid areas.

The most familiar species, the inland bearded dragon, *P. vitticeps*, is a spectacular lizard that has gone from comparative obscurity to pet shop availability in only a decade.

Description: The inland dragon is common over much of the arid and semiarid southeastern Australia. It is more robust than the eastern bearded dragon. In the wild it is found amid eucalypts, acacias, and brushlands, and on sandy and rocky plains. It may be seen basking and displaying from elevated rocks, tree trunks, and fence posts. The ground color varies from tan to gray to brick red, and usually blends well with the soils on which it is found. Broad, lighter paravertebral lines and some degree of dorsal blotching are usually present, although older males may be nearly unicolored.

Breeding: Young sexually mature inland dragon females can be amazingly prolific. They seem to cycle well using only a reduced winter photoperiod. Large, well-fed females may produce over 150 eggs a year (occasionally more than 35 a clutch). Fecundity decreases after the lizards attain five or six years of age, and may virtually end late in life. At an incubation temperature of 85°F,

incubation varies from just under two months to nearly three.

Two small "beardless" bearded dragons are also seen in American and European herpetoculture:

The (beardless) dwarf bearded dragon, *P. minor*, grows to just over a foot (30.5 cm). It is less popular in America than in Europe.

The second beardless species is the lesser bearded dragon. *P. brevis*. It is just slightly larger than the dwarf bearded dragon. You may see this lizard listed under two erroneous names: *P. "rankeni"* and *P. "henrylawsoni."* The common names of Rankin's dragon and Lawson's dragon are also often applied. The lesser bearded dragon comes from central Queensland, Australia.

Both of these small dragons breed well but produce fewer eggs than the larger species. Incubation techniques and durations are similar to those used for *P. vitticeps*.

Racerunners and Whip-tailed Lizards

The teiids, family Teiidae, are the New World counterparts of the lacertids, family Lacertidae. They are a very diverse group of lizards, more abundant in Latin than in North America.

Only about four genera are commonly seen in the pet trade and of these, the whiptails, racerunners, and tegus are the most familiar to hobbyists. They may be found both at reptile specialists and in neighborhood pet stores. (For information on tegus, the larger members of this group, see pages 73–75.)

Description: Husbandry for racerunners and whiptails is identical. The racerunners and whiptails are inherently nervous, quick to run/react to a perceived danger.

The highly attuned nervous system of racerunners and teiids makes them very adept at locating and grasping prey insects. Their eyesight, sense of touch, and sense of smell make it difficult for most insects to escape. Although not much work has been done on their hearing, racerunners and teiids probably also use their hearing in locating prey, because they pause, then use their front feet to quickly dig up an insect not visible from the surface. Circumduction is used to indicate nervousness or appeasement before a fast dash to safety and as a territorial signal to an interloping male.

There is a great deal of selection for teiids that recognize potential danger and quickly retreat. The dashes to safety are often along established trails, although whether the recognition of the trail is visual or by smell is unknown. These lizards use their digging skills to create burrows, with one being an extensive home burrow. Again, how they find their burrow to return to it is unknown.

Keeping: If you'd like to work with racerunners and whiptails there are a few conditions that must be met. They need to be kept suitably warm (a basking spot of 105 to 110°F [40.5–43°C] will be extensively utilized). Besides warmth, they should be provided with full-spectrum lighting, absolute dryness in the top levels of their substrate, sufficient and varied food, and several hiding areas. Their quarters should be spacious and uncrowded, with no more than a single male of the same (or closely related) species per enclosure. These are fast, nervous, wandering lizards, quick to stake out their territory and very quick to defend it. Provided with a natural photoperiod, they can be bred.

Breeding: Tropical whiptails and racerunners will cycle reproductively if provided with reduced humidity and day length in winter. All teiids are oviparous, and some of the smaller species—such as the checkered whiptail, *Aspidoscelis tesselatus* complex, are parthenogenic. The smaller species have a relatively few proportionately large eggs. Six-lined racerunners (northern populations of which probably need annual winter cooling to trigger breeding) lay three to six eggs; ameivas lay five (or fewer) eggs, and the rainbow racerunner, three eggs. Some specimens may double or even triple clutch.

Incubation length varies according to temperature and other factors. Our rainbow racerunner eggs, incubated at 90°F (32°C), hatched in about 52 days. Those incubated at 86°F (30°C) took 73 days to hatch, and fewer young emerged. A gravid imported *Ameiva ameiva* laid three eggs; a single egg hatched after 68 days of incubation.

Large and colorful, the giant ameiva, Ameiva ameiva, *a common species from Panama to Amazonian South America, is now established in Miami, Florida.*

Whiptails

Two color phases of the giant jungle runner, *A. ameiva*, originally from tropical Latin America, are well established in Miami, and indeed these Florida populations are now being harvested for the pet trade. This seems appropriate, because the introduction of this lizard is attributable to pet trade releases/rejects.

Description: The two phases are very different in appearance from each other. The charcoal gray and blue ameiva, the larger of the two, is called the jungle runner. Males may reach more than two feet (61 cm) in length. The second phase (the green-rumped whiptail) is pale yellow and green. The two races are geographically isolated from each other (pedestrian lizards have a harder time crossing Miami streets than humans!), and tend to stay well out of sight. Even in their localized population centers, their presence is more advertised by the rustling of grass as they retreat than by visual contact.

The green-rumped whiptail is sexually dimorphic. Males are noticeably larger—to 20 inches (51 cm)—than the females, and their coloration is tan-brown anteriorly, intensifying to blue-spangled lime-green posteriorly. Females are somewhat smaller, and less conspicuous in brown and russet, with some suffusion of green posteriorly. Those seen in Miami seem to glow in the intense sunlight.

Besides occurring in Latin America (and south Florida), other representatives of the genus Ameiva are found in the West Indies. On the island of Bimini, just east of Miami, *A. auberi richmondi* noses through debris under the Australian pines for tiny insects and snails. This wary 10-inch-long (25 cm) ameiva is blue and tan with a peach-colored nose.

Keeping/Breeding: See this discussion on pages 145–146 for information on keeping and breeding whiptails.

Two of the Latin American teiids now established in Miami, Florida, are Cnemidophorus lemniscatus, *the rainbow whiptail, and* Aspidoscelis motaguae, *the giant whiptail. The latter is the larger but less colorful of the two.*

Racerunners/Whiptails/ Rainbow Lizards

Description: As a group, these lizards are all pretty, and some are spectacular. Many are brown or tan, with light and/or dark stripes, spots, or a combination of both. Size ranges from eight inches (20 cm) to about a foot (30.5 cm) in overall length, two-thirds of which is tail. Cnemdophorines rest in an alert posture, with the head held up, away from the ground.

Members feed on insects, but most will consume fresh blossoms. Rainbow racerunners, *Cnemidophorus lemniscatus*, introduced from Colombia by the pet trade to the greater Miami area, often forage on the toxic European punctureweed, *Tribulus terrestris*, along with whatever insects they can find.

The male rainbow racerunners are showily clad in turquoise, lime green, old gold, and russet. Their brilliant appearance in the bright sunlight is impressive. The smaller females are less colorful, but display prominent dorsal stripes and have a reddish head.

Another new resident of the Dade County area is the Central American (also called Middle American) whiptail, *Aspidoscelis motaguae*. This 14 inch (35 cm) lizard has a russet head and tail, and the dorsum is liberally flecked with lemon yellow.

Besides eastern distribution of these two species, the arid and semi-arid areas of the western United States are home to at least 15 other species.

Keeping: Maintaining members of the genera *Cnemidophorus* and *Aspidoscelis* are addressed on pages 145–146, concerning all teiids.

Breeding: Sexuality could be said to be confusing in these lizards. Several species are "female only," and reproduction is parthenogenic. Other species are unisexual in some areas of their range and male-female in others. Still others are male-female throughout their range. Both the bisexual and unisexual forms use courtship or pseudo-courtship to stimulate egg development.

Chapter Eleven
The Woodland/Forest Terrarium

Woodland/forest terraria make suitable homes for lizards of humid temperate and tropical origins. Because so many kinds of potted house plants and formulated soils are available, these terraria are easily constructed and maintained. Branches and rocks from your yard can be used as both decorative and functional objects. The plants you install will need two things—adequate lighting and a drainage system that permits their roots to stay damp, not soggy.

For the substrate, start with an inch or two of pea-sized gravel. On top of the gravel lay a thickness or two of air conditioning filter material, cut to the exact size of terrarium—this will prevent the two inches to three inches (5.1 cm–7.6 cm) of soil that will be placed on top of the filtration material from filling the spaces between the gravel. The gravel serves as a reservoir that will prevent any excess water from destroying the roots of your plants if you happen to occasionally overwater.

A glass or plastic top over the tank will help retain the high humidity preferred by woodland lizards. If the humidity is too high, substitute a screen top.

Anoles

Description: There are more than 300 species of anoles in the world and more are being described regularly. About 125 species of anoles are of West Indian distribution, with all remaining species being found in North, Central, and South America. Only one species, the green anole, *A. carolinensis*, is native to the United States and, due to pet trade escapes, it is now established in Japan and other countries as well. Besides the green anole, which ranges widely over the lower elevations in the southeastern United States, another 11 species, all escapees from the American pet trade, are now firmly established in Florida. Among these are three impressively large species: the

Jamaican giant, *A. garmani*, the Marie-Galante Island sail-tailed, *A. ferreus*, and the Brobdignagian knight anole, *A. e. equestris*. While the first two of these large anole species push a foot (30.5 cm) in total length, the knight anole may attain (or slightly exceed) 18 inches (45.7 cm) in length.

Anoles are diurnal lizards. Most species are arboreal to some degree; some species persistently dwell in the tops of trees (canopy). Others may vary their habitat seasonally, dwelling in the canopy in the cooler or drier months but descending low on the trunks during hot, wet weather. The Marie-Galante, Jamaican giant, and knight anoles are among these latter, at least in their Florida range. Male anoles are usually the larger sex. Some species are capable of dramatic green to brown color changes; all species are capable of at least subtle color changes. The males of all, and the females of some, have distensible gular (throat) fans that are used in territoriality displays. The throat fans are also called dewlaps. In those species in which the females do have throat fans, the fans are proportionately smaller than those of the males. Most anoles also have expanded toetips with specialized subdigital lamellae that allow them to climb. Although most can traverse surfaces as smooth as glass, anoles are not as adept as some other lizards (most notably the geckos) at doing so.

The North American green anole is a species that is well known for its color changing abilities. An individual lizard may be brilliant green one minute and deep brown the next. The mechanisms that trigger these changes and the reasons the changes occur deserve mention.

Simply stated, the color changing results from the movement of pigment in the skin of the lizards. Stress (or comparative lack of it), rather than camouflage, is the motivating factor. Such things as fright, aggression, temperature, humidity, and light intensity all figure prominently in the color changes of these alert and visually oriented lizards.

When cool, basking green anoles are brown, a color that quickly absorbs heat. When warm, if in the open, the lizards are often a pale green; if in the shade, they may remain brown. If active, green anoles are often just that, a bright green. If involved in aggression, they are green but have a black patch behind each eye. Intermediate colors and combinations of browns and greens are not uncommon. Vague spots and streaks may appear and disappear on the back and sides. Heavily gravid females are particularly prone to this mottled color. Females often also have a light vertebral line. Over most of the range, the throat fan, present only in males of the green anole, is usually a pale pink. Some specimens in south Florida have white or pale cream throat fans.

Keeping: All of the anoles commonly encountered in the pet trade of America and Europe are well suited

Of the anoles, Anolis (Chamaeleolis) barbatus, *the Cuban bearded anole, is one of the most unique in appearance.*

for life in dry woodland terraria. Because these lizards vary widely in size, ranging from only a few inches (5–10 cm) to more than a foot and a half (45.7 cm) in overall length, the terrarium size will also need to vary to accommodate the species which you have decided to keep.

Breeding: Breeding receptivity of all anoles seems very distinctly affected by daylight length. With the increasing photoperiods of spring comes gonadal enlargement followed by display, courtship, and breeding. In most areas where anoles occur, the increasingly long photoperiods are accompanied by increasing warmth and relative humidity as well. These three factors seem to play a significant role in inducing captive anoles of all species to breed.

Although the green anole is primarily an insectivorous species, individuals may also lap at nectar,

pollen, tree-saps and actually consume an occasional brightly colored flower petal or two. Some learn to feed at hummingbird feeders.

As with all other anoles, the green anole is oviparous. From late spring, throughout the summer, the female lays a single (rarely, two) egg every two weeks. Each incidence of ovarian development is stimulated by a courtship sequence, but, since sperm retention is possible, not necessarily an actual breeding. The courtship includes head bobs, throat fan displays, and intricate body language (including "pushups").

Females do not usually prepare much of a nest. At best, the nest usually consists of shallow scrape only slightly deeper than the diameter of her eggs. As often as not, the egg(s) is/are merely placed in leaf litter, amid trash heaps, or in similar moisture-retaining sites. The female

Anolis e. equestris, the knight anole, is a Cuban lizard that has become established in southern Florida.

may or may not nudge the one or two eggs into the leaf litter with her nose. Incubation averages somewhat less than two months. Hatchlings are relatively large, often exceeding two inches (5.1 cm) in total length.

The knight anole, a native of Cuba, has been established in Florida for about three decades. The presence of Anolis equestris in that state results from several deliberate and many accidental introductions.

Description: Not only is the knight anole the largest species in Florida, it is the largest anole in the world. The 15-inch to 18-inch-long (38 cm–45.7 cm) adult males are truly impressive. (The spectacular A. smallwoodi, also of Cuba, is nearly as large.) The throat fans are present on both sexes and that of the male is of tremendous size. His fan reaches from the anterior lower lip to well back on the chest. When displaying (distending his throat fan in territorial dispute), knight anoles are at their very greenest. Green is also the most usual color for nondisplaying lizards. Besides green, knight anoles assume a yellowish, olive, deep brown, and many intermediate hues. In all colors, two light yellow-to-white flash marks are visible. The one on the shoulder is the most visible, and may be noticed when the lizard is otherwise hidden in the foliage. The second yellow marking is on the upper lip. It runs from eye to ear opening. Widely spaced, contrastingly colored crossbars are also occasionally present. Interstitial (between scale) skin is colored differently than the scales. When visible this may create a reticulated pattern of contrasting colors. The rear of the knight anole's head is more heavily casqued, and its head proportionately larger than that of any other U.S. anole species.

Knight anoles are highly arboreal, usually keeping well up in the canopy during cool weather, but descending to the trunks below the canopy when temperatures reach the high 80°s (30–32°C) and humidity is high. During midsummer knight anoles may descend to only a few feet above ground. There, low on the trunks, they assume a head-down resting/hunting position. Although knight anoles seem to prefer exotic foliage trees, we have also seen them on palms.

In comparison with smaller anole species, the knight anole is neither fast nor agile. In fact, when approached slowly and nonthreateningly, it will allow a person to come quite near before darting upward into the treetop. Also unlike its congenerics, most of which rely on agility to avoid danger, if cornered, knight anoles will stand their ground and can bite painfully hard. This fact has been attested to by many a collector. Typically, before biting, a knight anole will present itself broadside to the source of its displeasure, laterally flatten its body, open its mouth, extend the dewlap (at least somewhat), and erect a prominent nape and anterior vertebral crest.

Keeping: Knight anoles do best if kept in small groups (1 male to 2 or 3 females) in spacious, vertically oriented, well ventilated cages. They like a high cage humidity. Knight anoles are more omnivorous than the smaller species. Their large size also allows them great latitude in prey items. Insects, arthropods, other lizards, treefrogs, and fruit and berries are consumed. Larger examples of this large anole seem very fond of the fruit of the various Ficus (fig) trees that are grown as ornamental shade trees in Florida, and we have seen them feed on the ripe berries of Virginia creeper and poison ivy as well.

Breeding: Captive females deposit their clutches of one or two eggs in the leaf litter at the bottom of their cages. At ambient outdoor temperatures, incubation takes between 55 and 70 days. The hatchlings are quite dull in color. Female *equestris* lay several clutches and deposit more than a single clutch annually during the late spring and summer months.

The brown anole, *A. sagrei* ssp., is now one of the most frequently seen pet store species. A native of the West Indies, brown anoles are now nearly ubiquitous through the southern seven-eighths of the Florida peninsula, are common in the Lower Rio Grande Valley of Texas, and are now established in many parts of Latin America as well.

Description: Typical of most anoles, male sagrei are much the larger of the two sexes. Males approach a length of 8½ inches (21.6 cm). They are also of a darker color than the females. Female and juvenile brown anoles have a prominent dark-edged, scalloped (sometimes straight), light middorsal stripe. The throat fan color of the males may vary from yellow-orange to orange with a light border. When not distended, the border of the throat fan forms a light streak on the throat of the male lizard. Females lack the throat fan. Some males have rather well-developed tail crests. Erectile nuchal crests are well developed and an erectile vertebral crest is also usually present.

The brown anole is more terrestrial than any of our other anole species. It may be seen displaying amidst grasses, on sidewalks, and from clearing edges. Brush piles, dumps, and other litter-strewn areas may harbor large populations of brown anoles. Although brown anoles can and do climb, they are not as prone to ascend trees when frightened as other anoles. Instead, they often dart into or beneath available ground cover.

Keeping: If certain parameters are met, all anoles are rather easily kept and bred, and can be fairly long-lived.

To thrive, anoles must be kept warm, relatively humid, supplied with ample amounts of the correct food and drinking water, be given adequate vitamin/mineral supplements, and be provided with full-spectrum lighting and sufficient space. Males are very quarrelsome, and it is not a good idea to try to house more than one per enclosure.

Adequately sized caging is important. The smallest suggested terrarium for a pair of small species of anole would be a 20-gallon (75.7 L) capacity; a 50-gallon (189 L) capacity would be better. For the larger species, a 50-gallon (189 L) terrarium would be the smallest we would consider, and twice or three times that capacity would be far better. If

kept in outside cages (like many of our anoles, especially larger species, are), the smallest recommended cage size for small anoles is about 3 feet×2.5 feet×3 feet (91 cm×74 cm ×91 cm). A cage containing more than a pair of anoles should be about 3 feet×2.5 feet×5 feet (91 cm ×74 cm×152 cm).

A cage containing a pair or trio of Jamaican giant or knight anoles should measure about 4 feet×2.5 feet×5 feet (122 cm×74 cm×152 cm). A cage containing two pairs or trios should be about 6 feet×2.5 feet ×5 feet (183 cm×74 cm×152 cm).

If indoors the caging should be well illuminated, with heat lamps directed toward and warming horizontal and vertical perches. The vertical perches are important to the anole species (such as brown, Jamaican giant, and knight anoles) that preferentially position themselves head downward on vertical supports for basking and displaying. Both the heating and illumination can be provided by strategic placement of low wattage plant-grow or reptile-basking floodlights. In addition to the mostly non-UV-producing incandescent bulbs, a full-spectrum bulb should be used to provide ultraviolet light. As it does for all heliotropic (sun-basking) reptiles, UV-A promotes natural behavior and UV-B aids in the metabolism and utilization of vitamin D_3 and calcium. The UV-producing bulb should be no more than ten inches (25 cm) away from the basking area. It has rather recently been learned that ultraviolet rays are reflected from the extended dewlaps of some anole species, turning even the most blasé of yellows and buffs into spectacular displays. Now that this is known, research into UV perception as well as other aspects of the biology of these lizards is sure to follow.

Strive for an overall interior cage temperature of between 75 and 85°F (24–29°C). However, the temperature at the basking site(s) should average 92 to 95°F (33–35°C). If you are using a cage constructed of wood and wire, by moving the entire cage outdoors during the months of summer, you can take advantage of the best lighting and heating system of all—the sun! Do not move glass terraria into the sunlight; the glass will concentrate and intensify the heat, literally cooking your lizards within minutes.

Most anoles prefer to drink droplets of dew and rain from the leaves and branches amid which the lizards dwell. They are slow to recognize a dish of still water as a drinking source. We suggest that you grow live plants in your cages, and that you sprinkle or mist the leaves and enclosure thoroughly at least once a day. When the cages are indoors we do this carefully with a spray bottle. When the cages are outdoors we use the mist setting on the garden hose. This, of course, keeps the humidity within the cage high. Agitating the water in a dish by using an aquarium air stone will often enable an anole to perceive that this otherwise ignored source has drinking potential.

The crickets, giant mealworms, and waxworms that form the mainstay of the anole's diets are dusted with Osteoform or a similar multivitamin, or a calcium-D_3R additive twice weekly. We often alternate the treatment, using the Osteoform on Monday and the D_3 on Thursday. D_3 and vitamins are added to the food given to fast-growing baby anoles three or four times a week.

It can be hard getting some hatchling anoles to feed. This is especially true of some smaller species. We have found that pinhead crickets and termites are among the best accepted foods. Wingless fruitflies may also tempt holdout anoles to break their fast.

Although it is difficult to affix a "normal" captive lifespan to lizards that are most often collected from the wild as adults, we disagree with the commonly stated "two to four years" for smaller anole species. If endoparasite-free and cared for properly, a five-to-seven-year captive longevity is not uncommon for smaller anoles and larger species may exceed ten years. Some green anoles, A. carolinensis, have lived well over eight years. Now that some species are being captive bred, longevity records of more than a decade can be expected. The lives of these little lizards prove beyond any shadow of a doubt that herps neither need to be large nor exotic to be interesting and worthy of study.

Breeding: Female brown anoles expend little effort in nest preparation. The one (usually) or two (rarely) eggs are merely laid among plant debris, in a shallow scrape, on the ground beneath boards, cardboard, or other moisture-retaining material, and are produced at (about) 14-day intervals throughout the warm months. Incubation duration is variable, but may be as little as 45 or more than 60 days. The hatchlings, feisty from day one, do not hesitate to make cursory territorial displays at any perceived threat. Hatchling males distend their throats before the gular-fan has developed.

True Chameleons

Stated as simply as possible, true chameleons are not lizards that should be attempted by neophyte hobbyists. However, despite the fact that, as a group, chameleons are among the more difficult and demanding lizards to keep, hobbyists worldwide have a very real infatuation with them. The result is that many thousands of wild-caught chameleons, of species that are even more difficult than average to keep, are purchased by novice hobbyists annually. Among these are graceful, Senegal, and flap-necked chameleons (*Chamaeleo gracilis*, *C. senegalensis*, and *C. dilepis*, respectively). Sadly, few of these lizards remain alive for more than a few weeks or months. This is understandable when you consider how precise the captive care must be for even the hardiest species of chameleons and that those most

commonly imported are far from even moderately hardy. The species that have proven themselves most tolerant of captive conditions are the veiled, the Jackson's, and the panther chameleons (*C. c. calyptratus*, *C. jacksonii xantholophus,* and *Furcifer pardalis*, again respectively).

Because most pet store chameleons are stressed, wild-collected imported specimens, the health of which has already been compromised, we suggest you seek out and make your purchase from those few specialist reptile dealers, herpetoculturists, or fellow hobbyists who offer captive-bred and -born/hatched chameleons. To do well with *any* chameleon it needs to be as healthy and stress-free at the outset as possible.

Price alone will usually tell you what kind of a chance you will have at succeeding with the chameleon you choose. We'll use a generality here (and be the first to acknowledge that it is not always true) and state that if the chameleon is an adult and is selling for $35 or less, the chances are pretty good that it is a wild-caught specimen of one of the difficult-to-keep but easy-to-collect species. *Avoid it!* You'll be much further ahead if you spend twice or three times that much and purchase a captive-bred specimen of one of the three hardy breeds we've mentioned.

Although they are usually wild collected, the East African Jackson's chameleon, *C. jacksonii xantholophus,* and two Cameroon species, the four-horned and the mountain chameleons, *C. quadricornis* and *C. montium*, can, when suitable attention is given to details, usually be acclimated with some degree of success. It is important that you choose specimens that have not been too severely stressed by capture and shipping. The eyes should be protuberant with no encrustations, weight should be good, and coloration should be "normal." Chameleons of all species, stressed by any number of causes, often assume abnormally dark hues. If the dark colors continue for more than a few minutes, we do not consider these specimens good candidates for purchase.

Keeping: Chameleons do best if kept in spacious—not just *large*, but truly spacious—quarters. Although they are not one of the larger lizards, chameleons are best suited to heavily planted, vertically oriented, wire-covered, wood-framed terraria (cages). Ventilation is *very* important to their well-being.

We have always kept and bred our chameleons in walk-in cages—minimum size is 48 inches long × 30 inches wide × 60 inches high (122 cm × 76 cm × 152 cm) but are aware of breeding pairs surviving well in cages as small as 36 inches long × 24 inches wide × 24 inches high (91 cm × 61 cm × 61 cm).

To survive in captivity, chameleons require spacious, stress-free caging that is well ventilated (but *usually* humid). They also need an exemplary diet that (ideally) includes

The high elevation mountain chameleon, Chamaeleo montium, *is a relatively hardy captive.*

a variety of insects, ample hydration (most prefer to lick droplets of water from plants and terrarium walls), and comparative solitude.

Chameleons are not lizards that enjoy lizard company. If the cage is sufficiently large, and the species involved is one of the more tolerant species, a male and one or two females of the same species can coexist rather amicably. However, once bred, the females become more intolerant of the presence of a male. As a rule of thumb, if your cages are small, it is best to plan on keeping chameleons in solitary confinement except for short introductions of the female to the male's cage for the purpose of breeding.

Chameleons of most types do best when there are trees or sturdy shrubs in their cages. The lizards enjoy clambering in their sure-footed, hand-over-hand, method of moving along the limbs and trunks. We have found the small-leaved, sturdy *Ficus benjamina* or potted hibiscus to be among the better plant candidates. If these trees are left in their pots, the plants, with the lizards clinging to them, can be removed at cleaning time, and replaced when the chore is finished.

The presence of living plants in a chameleon cage also lends itself well to the ideal method of watering your chameleons. This is by spraying the plant and allowing droplets of water to form on the leaves and branches. This is easily accomplished with the mist nozzle on a hose when the cages are outside, but can also be done inside with a spray bottle. Even freshly imported chameleons, to which water intake is *very* important, will readily drink when water is provided in this manner.

A very few true chameleons are primarily terrestrial. These forms, among them Namaqua chameleons (*Chamaeleo namaquensis*), and the leaf chameleons (genera *Rhampholeon* and *Brookesia*), will prefer horizontally oriented terraria and should have their habitat requirements researched. Some will prefer sandy substrates; most will be more at home amongst a layer of dead leaves. All will climb on clumps of reindeer moss (lichen) or horizontal limbs and twigs.

Cage temperature is of particular importance to chameleons. While desert forms will naturally tolerate daytime highs near, or slightly above 90°F (32°C), such high temperatures will quickly stress forest-dwelling montane species like the ever popular Jackson's chameleons.

Chameleons do not enjoy being handled or restrained. Both of these acts can cause considerable stress. Assuring that chameleons are also comparatively parasite free (both external and internal parasites) is of extreme importance and assuring the latter will require veterinary assessment of fecal samples and should *never* be overlooked.

If it becomes necessary to actually lift a chameleon from its cage, be very careful when removing it from its perch. Chameleons will cling so tightly to twigs or wire that their claws can be pulled entirely out, or the tip of their prehensile tail seriously injured. Many chameleons can be shepherded onto a horizontally held twig or dowel far more easily than they can be lifted. This method of moving them is also less stressful for the lizards.

Feeding a chameleon the same kind of insect day in and day out can cause either of two kinds of problems: Either the chameleon will become so dependent on the insect that it will accept no other or the lizard will tire of the regularly offered insect and begin to feed reluctantly or cease feeding entirely. Neither of these results is desirable. We suggest that chameleons be fed as wide a variety of insects as possible and that if the insects are themselves captive raised that they be gutloaded (see page 41). Butterworms, king mealworms, crickets, and all manner of nonnoxious, freshly collected wild insects should be provided. In addition, several species of chameleons (the magnificent and hardy veiled chameleon being foremost among these) will avidly consume fresh greens and some other vegetables and blossoms.

Chameleons do not usually drink readily from dishes of standing water. Pendulous droplets of water clinging to plant leaves and branches are eagerly drunk. Regular misting or a drip system works well. If a dish is used, it will probably be necessary to roil the water with an aquarium air stone attached to a small vibrator pump. No matter what the system is, watch carefully to ascertain that your chameleon is drinking an adequate amount.

Dietary supplements of vitamin D_3 and calcium are important for all chameleons, and especially for fast-growing babies or ovulating/gestating females. Chameleons kept indoors will require more dietary calcium-D_3 supplementation than those kept outside. Care should be taken that vitamin A is not overdosed. It has been suggested by some herpetoculturists that goiter-like throat swellings that have affected some chameleons are directly or indirectly related to overdoses of vitamin A.

Breeding: Chameleons have large clutches and the process is stressful to females. You should assure that the female drinks copiously following deposition.

Live-bearing species bear their young in sticky membranous envelopes that adhere to branches and other objects. In low humidity situations, where the birth sacs can quickly dry, the young may need help escaping. Females of egg-laying species dig deep nests, often lay huge clutches, and are easily debilitated by the procedure. Sperm retention is well documented, and a female may continue to lay several clutches of fertile eggs after just a single mating. Eggs seem to develop best at "cool" temperatures; 74 to 80°F (23–27°C) seems ideal for most incubating eggs, but the eggs of montane species may do better if temperatures are a few degrees cooler.

Although many keepers advocate keeping their chameleons separately except for the purpose of breeding them, ours were always maintained in pairs or trios with no adverse effects whatever.

Veiled Chameleon

Description: Although the veiled chameleon comes from the desert countries of Yemen and Saudi Arabia, it comes from rather lush mountain slopes and riparian habitats that funnel and hold humidity. Thus, the veiled chameleon is not, in the strictest sense, a desert creature. There are two subspecies, but only the larger, more highly casqued form, *Chamaeleo c. calyptratus,* is commonly seen in American herpetoculture. Adult males, by far the larger sex, may near two feet (61 cm) in total length and have a

The beautiful veiled chameleon, Chamaeleo calyptratus, *is one of the hardiest of the chameleons in captivity. It is decidedly omnivorous.*

casque three or more inches (7.6 cm) in height. This species may be easily sexed from the moment it emerges from the egg. Males have a small but easily visible calcar (heel) spur on each hind foot. Normally active and unstressed males are clad in wide and well-defined bars of turquoise and brown on a blue-green to olive green ground color. Males involved in territorial displays are an intense turquoise and yellow. Non-gravid females (which they seldom are if adult) are green, with or without highlights of yellow, brown, or blue. Gravid or otherwise nonreceptive females become intensely patterned in orange (laterally) and turquoise (dorsally) on deep olive.

Keeping: While the lowland veiled and panther chameleons can easily withstand daily high temperatures in the upper 80°s or low 90s°F (31–33°C), montane species such as the Jackson's, mountain, and four-horned chameleons will not adapt to such warmth. These latter will do better if the daily highs are in the 70s°F (21–25°C) but should have a small area of a basking perch warmed to the low to mid 80s°F (26–29°C). This will furnish opportunity for thermoregulation.

Among plant species most favored by veiled chameleons (*C. calyptratus*, one of the most omnivorous species), are the leaves and blossoms of *Epipremnum* (=*Pothos*), *Syngonium*, *Ficus benjamina*, etc. Nasturtium, hibiscus, chopped escarole and romaine, and other such greens are also eaten.

Breeding: This is an oviparous species that, when captive, often has more than 30 eggs per clutch and several clutches a year. At 78 to 82°F (26–28°C), incubation of the eggs should take about eight months. The laying of eggs is an arduous process for the females. Although some withstand egg laying well, most become seriously dehydrated during the process. It is imperative that female chameleons be kept well hydrated at *all* times. Even with the most ideal of care, female veiled chameleons may weaken and die after two or three clutches have been laid.

Panther Chameleon

The Madagascar panther chameleon, *F. pardalis*, is far more variable in color than the veiled, but care, clutch size, and egg care are about the same for both. Some panthers may be turquoise banded with purple; some may be green banded with brown or blue or orange; some may be gaudily barred; others only vaguely so. Males occasionally attain a length of more than 20 inches (56 cm). Females are usually smaller and less colorful than the males, but if gravid, may be gaudily patterned with a series of fire-orange "portholes." Both sexes of one coveted morph are orange. Panthers have low but prominent casques. These are largest on adult males, which also have prominent hemipenial bulges at their tailbase.

Both the veiled and panther chameleons can tolerate daytime temperatures into the high 80°s (31–32°C) and easily withstand drops of up to 20 degrees at night.

Jackson's Chameleon

Males of the large Jackson's chameleon (*C. jacksonii xantholophus* is the largest and most commonly seen of the three subspecies) are horned like a triceratops. The females of this race usually lack horns. Males, which near 14 inches (36 cm) in length, may be bright to yellowish green (if the yellowish wash remains long it might indicate stress or illness!), often without many contrasting markings. Females are greenish with prominently contrasting bars of olive or other darker green. The bars are most complete dorsally, but may break into blotches laterally.

Understandably, this beautiful blue color phase of the Madagascar panther chameleon, Furcifer pardalis, *is eagerly sought by hobbyists.*

This is a high-altitude, live-bearing chameleon that thrives when ambient daytime temperatures don't go much above the very low 80s°F (27–28°C) (74 to 78°F [23–25.6°C] is better yet) and nighttime temperatures drop into the high 50s°F or

The horns of the male Mt. Kenya Jackson's chameleon, Chamaeleo jacksonii xantholophus, *are very well developed.*

low 60s°F (13.9–17°C). Jackson's chameleons will bask extensively to warm after a cold night, and may bask in a warmed hotspot at other times as well. Gravid females bask more regularly than non-gravid females or males do. Clutches may number from 5 to 50 babies, with from 10 to 25 being the most frequent numbers.

Interestingly, although the Jackson's chameleon is an East African species, those now available in the pet trade most often are collected from naturalized colonies in Hawaii.

Four-horned and Mountain Chameleons

Males of the high-altitude Cameroon four-horned, *C. quadricornis*, and mountain chameleons, *C. montium*, near a foot (30.5 cm) in length and are adorned with beautiful vertebral and caudal crests and prominent horns (two long ones in the case of the mountain and four shorter but easily seen plus two tiny ones in the case of the four-horned chameleon). Males are clad in scales of a beautiful new-leaf green, highlighted with yellowish, peach, and/or turquoise tints. Females of both are several inches smaller, of a darker green, and lack the cresting and the horns. Both lay up to a dozen eggs that, if incubated at about 71°F (21.7°C), will hatch in four and a half to six months. Nighttime temperatures in the 50s°F (10–14°C) and daytime temperatures in the low to mid-70°s F (21–23.9°C) are ideal. A hotspot for basking should be available.

Day Geckos

Although only eight or ten of approximately 60 species of day geckos are currently readily available in the pet trade, among them are some of the most beautiful of lizards. Despite being dubbed day geckos, these lizards are active both by day and night. A few species of day geckos occur in the Seychelles, the Comoros, on the islands of Reunion and Mauritius, on Round Island, and a single species occurs on the Andaman Islands in India's Bay of Bengal. However, on the island continent of Madagascar, the true diversity of day geckos can be seen. There, in all manner of habitats, from one end of the island

In comparison with the horns of many other chameleons, those of the Cameroon four-horned chameleon, Chamaeleo quadricornis, *are poorly developed.*

to the other, and on most of the surrounding islands, day geckos of one or more species occur. Conservationists fear that the long-term survival of many species is being threatened by rampant habitat destruction and that exportation of wild-collected day geckos for the pet trade is hastening the demise of many. True or not (and it probably is), since day geckos are very easy to breed, even casual hobbyist-breeders can help alleviate the collecting pressures on wild populations. At least one species, the gold dust day gecko, *P. laticauda,* is now firmly established in Hawaii and several species have been found on southern peninsular Florida. It is not known whether the Florida animals are established in feral breeding colonies or are merely unestablished escapees. Two large species, both now extinct, once occurred on the island of Rodriguez.

Description: The day geckos range in size from small (three inches [7.6 cm]—neon day gecko, *P. klemmeri*) to large (12 inches [30.5 cm]—Standing's day gecko, *P. standingi*) with most being somewhere between these two sizes. All have expanded toe tips, lidless eyes bearing round pupils, and most have a green (or at least greenish) ground color. A very few are brown or gray.

Males are more massive than females and have proportionately larger femoral pores. The pores can be easily seen by encouraging the gecko onto the glass side of a terrarium. The femoral pores continue

Small though they may be, peacock day geckos, Phelsuma quadriocellata, *are active, brilliantly colored, and hardy.*

uninterruptedly into the preanal area. Male day geckos also have slight hemipenial bulges at the base of the tail.

Day geckos are omnivorous, consuming not only insects but pollen, nectar, overripe fruits, and saps and juices as well. To truly thrive, captive day geckos require not only vitamin-mineral-dusted insects, but the "Phelsuma fruit-honey mixture," page 164.

Keeping: Although they were once considered difficult captives, in recent years a more throrough understanding of their needs has proven many species of day geckos hardy and long-lived. A great many species are now captive bred, and the availability of hatchlings from specialist breeders or dealers brings the number of species available up to about 25.

Hatchling day geckos of some species may look quite like the adults or may differ somewhat. This hatchling Madagascar giant day gecko, Phelsuma madagascariensis grandis, *bears a profusion of dark spots and blotches that will be lost with age.*

Phelsuma Fruit-Honey Mixture

An easily made and stored artificial diet for your day gecko consists of:

⅓ jar of mixed fruit or apricot strained baby food

⅓ jar of strained papaya baby food

1 teaspoon honey

⅓ eyedropper of Avitron liquid bird vitamins

½ teaspoon of Osteoform powdered vitamins

Add water to attain desired consistency

A small quantity of bee pollen can be added if it is available. Besides the vitamin-enhanced fruit mixture we provide our geckos with calcium-dusted crickets, waxworms, and an occasional giant mealworm. The size of the insects necessarily varies with the size of the geckos being fed. The three-inch-long (7.6 cm) neon day geckos require fly-sized (or smaller) crickets; the foot-long (30.5 cm) Standing's day geckos relish adults.

Day geckos are both territorial and easily stressed. Unless family groups (usually one male to one to four females) are established and compatible, and the cage conditions are suitable, day geckos may do poorly as captives. Although it is best to keep only one species (or subspecies) per cage, if cages are large enough, and sufficient visual barriers are provided, distantly related forms may be able to be housed in the same enclosure. It is not possible to keep males of closely allied species (Standing's, giant, etc.) in the same enclosure.

Since both males and females set up "pecking orders," it is particularly important to monitor the dynamics of the captive colony. Subordinate specimen(s) will continually hide, fail to feed properly, be continually fearful and nervous, and persistently display an abnormal coloration. You must know your geckos and be ready to take action to lessen the stress if it does become necessary. Continued stress can prove quickly fatal to an otherwise healthy gecko. Stress reduction can be accomplished in several ways: removing the lowest subordinate, adding visual

The neon day gecko, **Phelsuma klemmeri,** *is the smallest of the genus.*

barriers, or moving the entire group into a new and neutral terrarium.

Day geckos prefer to drink droplets of water from the leaves after the plants in their enclosure have been freshly misted.

Because of their remarkable brilliance and small size, most day geckos are considered by many hobbyists ideal candidates for inclusion in the tropical woodland terrarium. The size of the terrarium should be dictated by the adult size and the total number of the day geckos retained therein. Because they are persistently arboreal, day geckos do best in a "tall" terrarium. They do not tolerate crowding well. For a pair or trio of small to moderately sized geckos, a 15-gallon (56.8 L) "tall" tank will provide sufficient space. For a pair or trio of the large species, we suggest a minimum terrarium size (30 gallons [114 L]) and prefer a 50- to 80-gallon (189–303 L)

size. If constrained too tightly, day geckos may survive but won't thrive. A trio of Standing's day geckos that we have had for more than ten years now, has thrived and bred for five of those years in a 65-gallon (246.1 L) hexagonal terrarium in the corner of the living room. The tank is heavily planted, provided with several corkbark tubes and a large hollow log, and is well lit, having both a fluorescent fixture fitted with a Vita-Lite bulb and an incandescent "plant-grow" flood light. This latter provides warmth as well as illumination. Feeding stations for the honey-fruit mixture are on top of the log. To provide drinking water for the lizards the leaves of the plant are misted daily with tepid water. The substrate is merely four inches (10.2 cm) of sterilized potting soil.

When setting up a terrarium, incorporate both horizontal and vertical perches. Both seem neces-

Although not brightly colored as adults (top), hatchlings (bottom) of the large Standing's day gecko, Phelsuma standingi, are beautiful and coveted by hobbyists.

ing specimens of several day gecko species in outdoor walk-in cages of wood and wire construction (see pages 16–18). These cages have proven ideal.

The fondness of day geckos for sweets offers you a simple way of administering the necessary vitamin and mineral supplements as well. Without these latter, especially vitamin D_3 and calcium, day geckos are quite apt to develop a metabolic bone disorder (once simply called decalcification or rickets). Rapidly growing young and female geckos that are utilizing calcium to form the yolks and shells for their developing eggs will be affected more quickly than adult males or nonovulating females. Ideally, the ratio of calcium to phosphorus should be two or three to one. Vitamin D_3 is necessary to aid in the absorption and metabolism of the calcium. The use of vitamin/mineral supplements is necessary even with full-spectrum lighting.

As a group, day geckos are not easily handled. Their skin is extremely delicate, tearing easily if the lizards are inexpertly handled. Day geckos should be "cupped" (shepherded into a cup or jar that is then tightly covered after the lizard has entered) if it becomes necessary to remove them from their cages.

Breeding: The big grayish green Standing's geckos lay their eggs on the substrate inside the almost upright hollow log. The eggs adhere to each other but not to the substrate or the log. Thus, they are easily gath-

sary to the well-being of day geckos. Illuminate and warm at least one of the horizontal perches (preferably two) to provide a suitable basking area for your geckos. Sections of bamboo are ideal perch material. Horizontal tank length sections can be held in place by a dollop of latex aquarium sealant on each end. This will affix the bamboo to the glass.

Besides typical indoor glass terraria, we maintain additional breed-

ered up and incubated. The hard-shelled eggs are incubated in closed deli cups at a "moderate" relative humidity of 82 to 86°F (27.8–30°C), and hatch in about 60 days.

Emerald Tree Monitors

Description: The beautiful emerald, *V. prasinus*, is the most coveted of the tree monitors. It is a species of the lower elevations of Papua/New Guinea and of some of the surrounding islands. Often referred to merely as "emerald monitor," it is a long, lithe, prehensile-tailed species. Although some are considerably duller, most specimens of the emerald tree monitors have a leaf-green dorsum sparsely to profusely patterned with black. The pattern of the dark dorsal markings can vary from rearward directed chevrons to rather straight crossbars to an intricate reticulate pattern. Hatchlings are beautifully colored with jet black and the most brilliant of leaf green, often in nearly equal amounts. With the lizard's growth, the green quickly predominates.

This monitor rarely exceeds 30 inches (76 cm) in total length, of which somewhat more than 60 percent is slender prehensile tail. The tail prehensility is great enough to support the entire body weight of the monitor, if necessary. The tail is usually loosely coiled when the monitor is at rest, but may be coiled, equally loosely, around a branch when the lizard is active. The limbs of the emerald tree monitor are long and powerful and its toes are tipped with sharp, recurved claws.

Since these are rather small lizards, there is a tendency for one uninitiated in the handling of monitors to simply reach into the cage and grasp the monitor. To those of you so inclined we can say only one thing: *Don't!* Should you decide to ignore this admonition you will quickly find how decidedly uncomfortable the raking claws and strong jaws of this small, innocuous-appearing monitor can be. Besides scratching and leaving bloody welts, the emerald tree monitor will often also void its cloacal contents on your hand or arm. None of this is pleasant.

You will quickly find that safely handling an emerald tree monitor will take both of your hands. With one hand grasp the monitor firmly, immediately behind the head. Immobilize the forelimbs (folding them backwards) from above. Immediately grasp the rear of the body with your other hand, immobilizing and folding the rear legs backwards. If grasped only behind the head, the lizard will arc its body and severely rake your arm and hand with its rear claws.

With perseverance on the part of their keeper, emerald tree monitors can become somewhat accustomed to handling. Admittedly, getting them to that point can be frustrating. We have always considered these lizards only a display animal, taking our pleasure from the beauty,

Emerald tree monitors, Varanus prasinus, *may be prominently banded with black or virtually a uniform green.*

and quasi-natural actions of the animal in its lushly planted woodland terrarium.

Keeping: Emerald tree monitors are coveted by private collectors and zoos alike. Once diagnosed and treated for any endoparasites and provided with a spacious cage (we strongly feel that these active arborealists should not be tightly confined!) and suitable temperature and humidity, most emerald monitors will prove quite hardy.

Although most will accept small mice as prey, we feel that a varied diet is much better for the lizards. Ours have eaten crickets, grasshoppers, June beetles (easily collected around porch lights in the spring), and king mealworms in addition to baby mice. Some tree monitors will also accept an occasional strip of

lean beef, good quality canned cat food, and monitor ration. Large slugs were especially relished by some tree monitors that we maintained. After eating one of these slimy creatures, the monitors would laboriously wipe the sides of their mouth against branches and leaves in an attempt to remove the copious amount of slime left there by the slug.

A daytime thermal gradient of from about 84 to 92°F (28.9–33°C) with a relative humidity of 75 percent plus is satisfactory. A nighttime temperature of 68 to 75°F (20–24°C) is satisfactory and no thermal gradient is necessary.

Emerald tree monitors should be housed in a tall cage and provided with a number of suitably sized limbs on which to climb. They are shy lizards that fully utilize the hiding places provided by growing plants, securely affixed hollow limbs, or even cockatiel nesting boxes. When their cage habitat is being built, elevated basking limbs accessed by a diagonally affixed tree trunk, should also be provided. Some keepers prefer flat plywood shelves to limbs, but we have found the plywood more difficult to keep clean and odorless. We provide an individual basking perch at about the same level for every emerald in any cage. This will often provide a degree of harmony not possible if the dominant specimen is attempting to restrict access of subordinate specimens to a single desirable basking limb. A basking hotspot— 95 to 98°F (35–36.7°C)—should be provided on each perch. When multiple bulbs are used to provide several warmed basking areas, care must be taken that the cage does not become overheated.

Emerald tree monitors naturally harbor large quantities of endoparasites that, in conjunction with dehydration and the other stresses related to shipping, can rather quickly cause the death of a freshly imported specimen. This is true even if the lizard is feeding well. Emerald tree monitors will usually rehydrate well in a hydration chamber (pages 32–33). Stool samples should be analyzed by a qualified veterinarian and a specific parasiticide given the lizard, if necessary.

We consider emerald tree monitors a species for the advanced hobbyist, and only then if you are willing to address and accommodate its many needs.

Breeding: Emerald monitors are very difficult to sex. Manual eversion of the hemipenes can be accomplished on hatchling specimens but some adult males will evert their hemipenes if restrained. Should a restrained monitor not evert its hemipenes, you must then wonder whether you are holding a female that has no hemipenes to evert or a male that doesn't choose to evert his. Gentle probing, although still controversial with monitors, does seem to work rather well with this species. Males, of course, probe more deeply than females.

To date, captive breedings of this remarkable monitor have been infrequent, but not unknown. The emerald tree monitor has been bred by several zoos and by private hobbyists as well. It seems that more success is being had in Europe than in the United States. The reported clutches are small, numbering from as few as two, to five, eggs.

At 86°F (30°C), the incubation takes slightly less than five months and hatchlings vary from a reported 3½ inches (8.9 cm) to well over 5 inches (12.7 cm) in total length. If proper care is given, the growth of this monitor is rapid. A subadult size can be attained within the first year. It remains unknown at what age sexual maturity is attained, but it is probably not until two or even three years of age.

Chapter Twelve
The Semiaquatic Terrarium

The semiaquatic terrarium is fairly simple to set up, but when used for water-going lizards, problems quickly arise. Remember that semiaquatic life in the wild differs from the much smaller world of a semiaquatic terrarium. In the wild a lizard can swim, then bask and dry off in the sun. Unless the semiaquatic terrarium consists of a wood and wire cage set up outside in a subtropical or tropical region, such basking will be denied the lizard. High humidity and a chronic inability to dry thoroughly can quickly cause skin problems that only get worse. The end result is a dead lizard.

Semiaquatic terraria can be beautiful when properly arranged. A few lizards, such as the water dragons and the basilisks, will do well if these tanks are spotlessly maintained.

There are several ways to set up a semiaquatic terrarium, but we will describe only one way that minimizes the maintenance required.

In this type of tank, land is layered as in the woodland terrarium, using gravel, A/C filtration material, and the topsoil. The water is contained in a suitably sized plastic dish sunk to its rim in the topsoil. To clean, you just lift out the water dish, empty and sterilize it, then replace and refill it.

The intricacy of the plantings and land design of the terraria are limited only by your imagination and available funds.

Water Dragons

The water dragons, *Physignathus*, are beautiful water-loving lizards found along river systems in southeast Asia and in Australia. These moderate-sized lizards are generally thought to be less nervous than basilisks, but, in all honesty, there's not much difference in nervousness between wild-caught adults of either type. Both will batter their noses against the sides of their cages in an effort to escape. It is better, whenever possible, to acquire captive-

Male green water dragons, Physignathus cocincinus, *near 2 feet (61 cm) and length and are powerful swimmers.*

hatched specimens, or at least immature wild-collected specimens. Young specimens of either the green or the brown water dragon tame better, or at least quiet down more, than adults.

Both species of water dragons are now being extensively bred in captivity, but wild-collected specimens of the southeast Asian green water dragon, *P. cocincinus*, are imported in large numbers. The ready availability of the green water dragon is reflected in its prices, even for captive-bred specimens.

In contrast, the protected status of the Australian brown water dragon, *P. lesueuri,* means few are available in the pet trade. Their relative rarity insures that they will continue to sell for high prices for a few more years.

Description: The two species of water dragon can be easily differentiated from each other. The green water dragon, *P. cocincinus*, is of some shade of green dorsally, with a vertebral crest extending from the nape of the neck to the tail base. The actual shade of green varies by population and degree of stress (or lack of stress) being felt by the lizard. Stress, as used here, may indicate one or a combination of factors, including adverse temperatures, physical restraint, endoparasitism, territorial encroachments by other lizards, or fright. (Dominant, sexually active, male green water dragons are often a very bright shade of green, with perhaps a yellow or peach suffusion anterio-ventrally.)

Body bands, when present, are light; tail bands (almost always

Adult male northern brown basilisks, Basiliscus vittatus, *bear a prominent head crest but lack vertebral and caudal crests. This species is now abundant in quiet waterways near Miami, Florida.*

prominent, especially on the distal two-thirds of the tail) are dark. Although both sexes bear the crest, that of the male is much larger. When dominant males are indulging in territorial displays, the crest is prominently raised.

With a distribution over much of southeast Asia, green water dragons are more exclusively tropical, hence more cold-sensitive than their brown cousins. Most of the green water dragons currently available are from Vietnam. These specimens seem to be a little darker in coloration as well as a little smaller than those once imported from Thailand.

Keeping: It would appear that water dragons are primarily carnivorous and insectivorous in the wild but may consume a little fruit and a few flowers as well. In captivity they readily accept small mice, canned cat foods, insects, and some fruits, flowers and vegetables.

Breeding: Both species are oviparous. Females dig deep nests in which they deposit from 8 to 14 eggs. At 86°F (30°C) the eggs hatch in from 72 to 90 days. It seems as if a period of hibernation is necessary to cycle the brown water dragon productively.

Basilisks

The tropical American members of the genus *Basiliscus* are frequently seen in captivity. Of the four species, it is the very beautiful green basilisk, *B. plumifons*, that most hobbyists and herpetoculturists favor. Not only is this species the most brilliantly colored of the genus, but the males have the most prominent cresting as well.

Male green basilisks, Basiliscus plumifrons, *bear two crests on their head plus prominent vertebral and caudal crests.*

The green basilisk is a species of forest-pool, marsh, and swamp edges. It ranges from Guatemala to Costa Rica.

Until recently, green basilisks have been only sporadically available to the pet trade. Currently, however, not only are large numbers of these lizards being collected and imported from Nicaragua, but captive breeding successes are now providing very large numbers of hatchlings to hobbyists. The hatchlings have proven hardy and easily reared.

Description: Adult males of the green basilisk have finlike crests on the back and tail and a double crest on the head. It is from the narrow, plumelike anterior cranial crest that the vernacular of "plumed basilisk" and specific name of "plumifrons" is derived.

The ground color is green (varying from light to dark), often with blue lateral spots and some vertical black markings in the vertebral crest. The iris is brilliant orange-yellow.

Adult males attain a length of more than 28 inches (71 cm). Adult females are several inches smaller.

At best, basilisks are nervous lizards. If startled they may dash wildly into the sides of the terrarium. Over time this flight reaction can cause severe nose (rostral) damage. Wild-collected basilisks are even more nervous than captive-bred and -hatched specimens. Strangely, females are often noticeably calmer than males. This is even apparent in the field, where females and juveniles may allow a fairly close approach, but males will dash away at the slightest movement.

Keeping: With some particularly nervous captives, it may be necessary to cover most of the glass of a basilisk terrarium with an opaque paper (or other such material) to prevent frightening the lizards.

Dietary studies seem still in order with this species. Despite the fact that green basilisks live well and are rather easily bred, over time there is a noticeable tendency for captive specimens to lose some intensity of color. Perhaps a higher concentration of dietary Betacarotenes would reverse this trend.

When kept in a semiaquatic terrarium, it is important that basilisks be provided with the opportunity to completely dry off and to bask in the warmth of a heat lamp. As mentioned before, if forced to remain perpetually wet, skin disorders can occur.

Except in large and heavily planted tanks, the nervous activity of large basilisks is apt to keep your arrangement in perpetual disarray. The problem is not so great with small specimens. Yet, despite the potential problems, the beauty of these lizards make the special considerations well worthwhile.

Breeding: A healthy, properly cycled, female green basilisk may have up to three clutches of eggs in a single season of breeding. The nest will be dug at the base of a plant or log in moist sand/soil substrate. Eggs may number from 6 to 16 per clutch. At an incubation temperature of 84 to 86°F (29–30°C) the eggs hatch in slightly more than two months.

Resources

Lizards that once were rare in the private sector and an ever-increasing number of caging designs and support materials are available in today's pet market. To find a particular lizard species, a specific terrarium or cage design, or the newest materials available, look in the following periodicals:

Reptiles Magazine
P.O. Box 6050
Mission Viejo, CA 92690

Herpetological/herpetocultural clubs can be found in many cities. Check with the biology department of your nearest university, or with the personnel of nature centers or museums to find the location of the club nearest you.

International clubs and societies with interests in particular lizard families also abound. Many have their own informative newsletters and bulletins.

Additional Reading

Even when a book of this type covers a specific group of lizards, there is always need for additional reading and research. The fact that we have covered myriad subjects and groupings in these pages merely accentuates the need. We suggest the following books to those readers seeking additional information on a particular subject.

Arnold, E. N. and J. A. Burton. *A Field Guide to the Reptiles and Amphibians of Britain and Europe.* London: Collins, 1978.

Bartlett, R. D. and Patricia Bartlett. *Iguanas, A Complete Pet Owner's Manual.* Hauppauge, NY: Barron's Educational Series, Inc., 2003.

_____. *Chameleons, A Complete Pet Owner's Manual.* Hauppauge, NY: Barron's Educational Series, Inc., 2005.

_____. *Geckos, A Complete Pet Owner's Manual.* Hauppauge, NY: Barron's Educational Series, Inc., 2005.

_____. *Monitors and Tegus, A Complete Pet Owner's Manual.* Hauppauge, NY: Barron's Educational Series, Inc., 2006.

_____. *Anoles, Basilisks, and Water Dragons, A Complete Pet Owner's Manual.* Hauppauge,

NY: Barron's Educational Series, Inc., 2008.

Branch, Bill. *A Field Guide to the Snakes and Other Reptiles of Southern Africa*. Sanibel, FL: Ralph Curtis Publishing, 1988.

Cei, J. M. *Reptiles del centro, centro-oeste y sur de la Argentina*. Torino: Museo Regionale di Scienze Naturali, 1986.

Cogger, Harold A. *Reptiles and Amphibians of Australia*. Ithaca: Cornell, 1992.

Conant, Roger and Joseph T. Collins. *Reptiles and Amphibians, Eastern/Central North America*. New York: Houghton Mifflin, 1991.

Donoso-Barros, Roberto. *Reptiles de Chile*. Santiago: Universidad de Chile, 1964.

Frost, Darrel R. and Richard Etheridge. *A Phylogenetic Analysis and Taxonomy of Iguanian Lizards* (Reptilia: Squamata). Lawrence: University of Kansas, 1989.

Frye, Fredric L. *Husbandry, Medicine, and Surgery in Captive Reptiles*, 2nd Ed. Malabar, FL: R. E. Kreiger Publ. Co., 1991.

_____. *Iguanas: A Guide to Their Biology and Captive Care*. Malabar, FL: R. E. Kreiger, 1993.

Glaw, Frank and Miguel Vences. *A Field Guide to the Amphibians and Reptiles of Madagascar*. Bonn: Privately Published, 1994.

Halliday, Tim and Kraig Adler. *The Encyclopedia of Reptiles and Amphibians*. New York: Facts on File, 1986.

Hunziker, Ray. *Leopard Geckos, Identification, Care, and Breeding*. Neptune City, NJ: TFH, 1994.

Jes, Harald. *Lizards in the Terrarium, A Complete Pet Owner's Manual*. Hauppauge, NY: Barrons Educational Series, Inc., 1987.

Le Berre, François. *The Chameleon Handbook*. Hauppauge, NY: Barron's Educational Series, Inc., 2000.

Levell, John P. *A Field Guide to Reptiles and the Law*. Excelsior, MN: Serpent's Tale Books, 1995.

Minton, S.A. *A Contribution to the Herpetology of West Pakistan*. NYC: Bulletin of the American Museum of Natural History, 1966.

Obst, Fritz Jurgen, et al. *The Completely Illustrated Atlas of Reptiles and Amphibians for the Terrarium*. Neptune City: TFH, 1988.

Schmidt, W., et al. *Chameleons, Vols. 1 and 2*. Neptune City: TFH, 1994.

Schwartz, Albert and Robert W. Henderson. *Amphibians and Reptiles of the West Indies*. Gainesville, FL: University of Florida Press, 1991.

Seuffer, Herman. *Keeping and Breeding Geckos*. Neptune City: TFH, 1985.

Slavens, Frank and Kate Slavens. *Reptiles and Amphibians in Captivity: Breeding, Longevity, and Inventory*, Current January 1, 1993. Seattle: Slaveware, 1993.

Smith, Hobart M. and Edward H. Taylor. *Herpetology of Mexico*. Ashton, MD: Eric Lundberg, 1966.

Both a high casque and a beard are typical of the high-casqued chameleon,
Chamaeleo hohnelii.

Smith, Malcolm A. *The Fauna of British India, Reptilia, and Amphibia*. Vol. II Sauria. Hollywood, FL: Ralph Curtis Books, Reprint 1973.

Stebbins, Robert C. *A Field Guide to the Western Reptiles and Amphibians*. Boston: Houghton Mifflin, 1985.

Walls, Jerry G. *Skinks: Identification, Care, and Breeding*. Neptune City: TFH, 1994.

Wright, John W. and Laurie J. Vitt (Editors). *Biology of Whiptail Lizards*. Norman, OK: Oklahoma Museum of Natural History, 1993.

Zhao, Er-Mi and Kraig Adler. *Herpetology of China*. Oxford, OH: SSAR, 1993.

Zimmerman, Elke. *Breeding Terrarium Animals*. Neptune City: TFH, 1983.

Glossary

Aestivation A period of warm weather inactivity; often triggered by excessive heat or drought.

Allopatric Not occurring together but often adjacent.

Ambient temperature The temperature of the surrounding environment.

Anterior Toward the front.

Anus The external opening of the cloaca; the vent.

Arboreal Tree-dwelling.

Autotomize The ability to break easily or voluntarily cast off (and usually to regenerate) a part of the body. This is used with tail-breakage in lizards.

Axillary Near the apex (pit) of the arm.

Bicuspid As used here, pertaining to claws with two points.

Brille The clear spectacle that protects the eyes of lidless-eyed geckos and other lizards.

Brumation The reptilian and amphibian equivalent of mammalian hibernation.

Canthus rostralis (canthal crest) A ridge from beneath the eye to the snout. This may be sharply or gently angled from the plane of the snout.

Casque The upward projecting cap or helmet at the back of a lizard's head.

Caudal Pertaining to the tail.

Chromatophore A skin cell that contains pigment.

Cloaca The common chamber into which digestive, urinary, and reproductive systems empty and that itself opens exteriorly through the vent or anus.

Con... As used here, a prefix to several words (generic, specific) indicating "the same." (Congeneric refers to species in the same genus; conspecific indicates the same species.)

Crepuscular Active at dusk or dawn.

Deposition As used here, the laying of the eggs.

Deposition site The spot chosen by the female to lay her eggs.

Dermal Relating to the skin.

Diapause A temporary cessation of development, often induced by coolness or dryness.

Dichromatic Two color phases of the same species, often sex-linked.

Digit Finger/Toe

Dimorphic A difference in form, build, or coloration involving the same species; often sex-linked.

Diurnal Active in the daytime.

Dorsal Pertaining to the back; upper surface.

Dorsolateral Pertaining to the upper sides.

Dorsum The upper surface.

Endemic Confined to a specific region.

Endolymphatic sacs The sacs of calcium carbonate located on both sides of the neck in certain members of the subfamily Gekkoninae.

Femoral pores Openings on the underside of the thighs of lizards. These pores produce a waxy exudate.

Femur The part of the leg between hip and knee.

Flanks Lower side.

Form An identifiable species or subspecies.

Fracture planes Softer areas in the tail vertebrae that allow the tail to break easily if seized.

Genus A taxonomic classification of a group of species having similar characteristics. The genus falls between the next higher designation of "family" and the next lower designation of "species." Genera is the singular of genus. The generic name is always capitalized when written.

Glossohyal A muscle of the extensible tongue.

Granular Pertaining to small, flat scales.

Gravid The reptilian equivalent of mammalian pregnancy.

Gular Pertaining to the throat.

Gular crest A longitudinal ridge of enlarged throat scales.

Heliothermic Pertaining to a species that basks in the sun to thermoregulate.

Hemipenes The dual copulatory organs of male lizards and snakes. Singular form: hemipenis.

Heterogenous Not uniformly sized, colored, or patterned.

Homogenous Uniformly sized, colored, or patterned.

Horns As used here, referring to the tapered, rigid, often annulated, forward projecting preocular or rostral processes.

Hybrid Offspring resulting from the breeding of two species.

Hydrate To restore body moisture by drinking or absorption.

Insular As used here, island-dwelling.

Intergrade Offspring resulting from the breeding of two subspecies.

Juvenile A young or immature specimen.

Keel A ridge (along the center of a scale).

Keratin The hardened, largely inert, protenaceous outer skin of a reptile.

Labial Pertaining to the lips.

Lamellae The transverse scales that extend across the underside of a gecko's toes.

Lateral Pertaining to the side.

Malagasy Republic Madagascar

Melanism A profusion of black pigment.

microhabitat The precise niche in which a lizard dwells.

Middorsal Pertaining to the middle of the back.

Midventral Pertaining to the center of the belly or abdomen.

Hemitheconyx taylori, *Taylor's fat-tailed gecko, is a very poorly understood gecko that has proven difficult to acclimate.*

Monotypic Containing but one type.

Nocturnal Active at night.

Occipital lobe The flaps or lobes of skin at the rear of some chameleons' heads.

Ocelli Light-centered rings.

Ontogenetic changes Changes occurring during growth.

Ontogeny The course of development.

Oviparous Reproducing by means of eggs that hatch after laying.

Ovoviviparous Reproducing by means of shelled or membrane-contained eggs that hatch prior to, or at deposition.

Parietal eye A sensory organ present in certain reptiles that is positioned midcranially.

Phalanges The bones of the toes.

Poikilothermic A species with no internal body temperature regulation. The old term was "cold-blooded."

Polymorphic More than one color phase.

Posterior Toward the rear.

Preanal pores A series of pores, often in the shape of an anteriorly directed chevron, and located anterior to the anus.

Prehensile Grasping.

Preocular Anterior to the eye.

Race A subspecies.

Rostral Pertaining to the nose area.

Rugose Not smooth; wrinkled or tuberculate.

Saxicolous Rock-dwelling.

Scansorial Capable of, or adapted for climbing.

Serrate Saw-like.

Setae The hairlike bristles in the lamellae of a gecko's toes.

Spatulae The flattened distal ends of the setae.

Species A group of similar creatures that produce viable young when breeding; the taxonomic designation that falls beneath genus and above subspecies.

Subdigital Beneath the toes.

Subspecies The subdivision of a species; a race that may differ slightly in color, size, scalation, or other criteria.

Sympatric Occurring together.

Tarsal spur An outgrowth on the heel.

Taxonomy The science of classification of plants and animals.

Terrestrial Land-dwelling.

Thermoregulate To regulate (body) temperature by choosing a warmer or cooler environment.

Thigmothermic Pertaining to a species (often nocturnal) that thermoregulates by being in contact with a preheated surface such as a boulder or tarred road surface.

Tuberculate Pertaining to tubercles.

Tubercles Warty protuberances.

Tympanum The external eardrum.

Vent The external opening of the cloaca; the anus.

Venter The underside of a creature; the belly.

Ventral Pertaining to the undersurface or belly.

Some of the small Savasin's giant geckos bear a light chevron on the nape.

Ventrolateral Pertaining to the sides of the venter (belly).

Vertebral Pertaining to the mid-dorsal area.

Vertebral crest A ridge of scales or an actual longitudinal middorsal crest.

Note: Other scientific definitions are contained in the following two volumes:

Peters, James A. *Dictionary of Herpetology*. New York: Hafner Publishing Co., 1964.

Wareham, David C. *The Reptile and Amphibian Keeper's Dictionary*. London: Blandford, 1993.

Index

Numbers in **bold** refer to pictures.